NORTHWEST HOMEGROWN COOKBOOK SERIES

Wild Mushrooms

CYNTHIA NIMS

ILLUSTRATED BY DON BARNETT

WestWinds Press®

I dedicate this volume of the series to the intrepid souls who brave the

uncharted paths and damp, chill conditions of Northwest forests to bring the timeless

taste of wild things into our modern lives of convenience. Authors, educators, foragers,

chefs—through their particular fondness for wild mushrooms, we all are

reminded to appreciate the uncultivated culinary gems of our region.

Text © 2004 by Cynthia Nims
Illustrations © 2004 by Don Barnett
Published by WestWinds Press®
An imprint of Graphic Arts Center Publishing Company
P.O. Box 10306, Portland, Oregon 97296-0306
503/226-2402; www.gacpc.com

Disclaimer: This book is not intended in any way to serve as a handbook for wild mushroom foraging. Neither the author nor the publisher is responsible for any allergic or other adverse reactions the reader may have when eating wild mushrooms.

Library of Congress Cataloging-in-Publication Data

Nims, Cynthia C.
  Wild mushrooms / Cynthia Nims ; illustrated by Don Barnett.
    p. cm. — (Northwest homegrown cookbook series)
Includes bibliographical references and index.
  ISBN 1-55868-695-9 (softbound)
1. Cookery (Mushrooms) 2. Mushrooms. I. Title. II. Series.
  TX804.N55 2004
  641.6'58—dc22   2003027551

President: Charles M. Hopkins
Associate Publisher: Douglas A. Pfeiffer
Editorial Staff: Timothy W. Frew, Tricia Brown, Kathy Howard, Jean Andrews, Jean Bond-Slaughter
Production Staff: Richard L. Owsiany, Susan Dupere
Editor: Ellen Wheat
Designer: Elizabeth Watson

Printed in Hong Kong

Mention of the Pacific Northwest evokes powerful imagery, from the region's rugged ocean coast to massive mountain peaks, dense forests, and lush valleys, and to the rolling hills beyond. This topography along with dynamic Pacific weather patterns create the climate that, in turn, drives our seasonal rhythms—indeed, four distinct seasons. From the damp, mild coastal areas to the more extreme arid land east of the Cascade Mountains, the Northwest boasts a range of growing regions that yield a boggling array of foods. The Northwest—from Alaska and British Columbia to Washington, Idaho, Oregon, and Northern California—is a top national producer of apples, lentils, hops, hazelnuts, plums, peppermint, sweet onions, potatoes, and many types of berries. The ocean, bays, and rivers supply the region with a broad selection of fish and shellfish, and rain-soaked foothills give us prized wild mushrooms.

For the Northwest cook, this wealth of ingredients means ready access to mouthwatering edibles such as morels and asparagus with halibut in the spring, rich salmon with peaches and raspberries during summer, delicious pears, chanterelles, and cranberries harvested in the fall, and plump oysters and mussels in winter.

The distinctive bounty of our regional foods makes for a culinary landscape that is as compelling as the natural landscape. This series of *Northwest Homegrown Cookbooks* shines the spotlight on those individual foods that flourish seasonally in this place that I call home. Savor this taste of the Northwest.

ACKNOWLEDGMENTS

One of the joys of being a writer is that each new project offers a world of new things to learn. For this book, a whole slew of people served as outstanding teachers about the world of wild mushrooms. They include Fred Rhoades, Ph.D., lecturer at Western Washington University and mycology consultant; Veronica Williams on the Long Beach Peninsula, Washington; David Campiche and Lori Anderson, owners of the Shelburne Inn, Long Beach Peninsula; Tony and Ann Kischner, owners of the Shoalwater Restaurant, Long Beach Peninsula; Patrice Benson from the Puget Sound Mycological Society; Jack Czarnecki from the Joel Palmer House in Dayton, Oregon; Dr. Charles Lefevre of New World Truffieres in Oregon; David Wheeler from Oregon White Truffles; Bob Engel and John Guardino at Gourmet Mushrooms, Inc., in Sonoma County, California; Heidi Cusick and Alan Kantor in Mendocino, California; Bill Jones on Vancouver Island, British Columbia; and Elaine Corets on the Olympic Peninsula, Washington.

Many thanks to David Arora for his input both in person and by way of his treasured resources, *Mushrooms Demystified* and *All That the Rain Promises, and More . . . .* I felt like I was meeting a rock star when I went on a foray with him at the Mendocino Wine and Mushroom Fest.

Leora Bloom's keen eye for detail and gracious, upbeat manner proved a great help with so much of this book.

I so appreciate Jeremy Trumble and John Gibbs at The Inn on Orcas Island, in Washington's San Juan Islands, for providing a much-needed writing retreat.

And finally, thanks to the testing troupe—Michael Amend, Jeff Ashley, Cathy Sander, Barbara Nims, Ed Silver, Paul Swanson, Shannon Borg, and Tim Kehrli—and the dedicated diners who help polish the recipes to be their best.

Chanterelles

Cantharellus cibarius

Cantharellus subalbidus

Craterellus cornucopioides

CONTENTS

Breakfast/Brunch 17

Appetizers 29

Soups, Salads, and Side Dishes 49

Main Courses 63

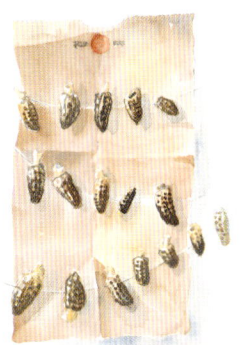

Cooking with Wild Mushrooms 86

The Story of Northwest Wild Mushrooms

Those Delectable Wild Edibles

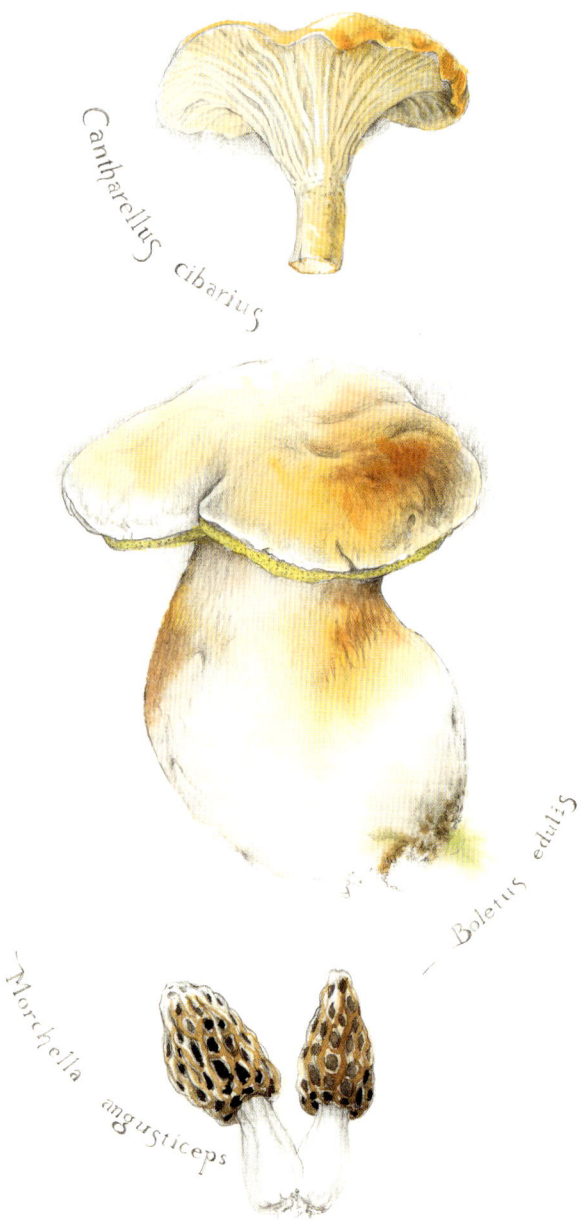

Cantharellus cibarius

Boletus edulis

Morchella angusticeps

The range of flavors and textures that wild mushrooms offer ranks these gems among the most celebrated culinary treats in the world. We in the Pacific Northwest are generously blessed by the selection of wild mushrooms available in our region. The edible mushrooms of the Northwest— as many as fifty species by some accounts— thrive in a range of growing areas, from sea-level fields to undergrowth in mountain foothills to higher subalpine elevations. In addition, the fact that there is such a variety of microclimates from Northern California into Alaska means that the seasonal selection of wild mushrooms varies from region to region as well as from month to month. Weather, too, is a significant variable—a damp August one year, a near-drought the next, early October frosts—impacting the availability of different mushroom types. Generally, wild mushrooms live up to their "wild" nature, proving fascinating and unpredictable but so delectable as to be worth the patience and flexibility required of the cook.

While perhaps a couple dozen types of mushrooms may be harvested for commercial distribution in the region, four species reflect by far the bulk of that harvest, both in volume and in cash value: chanterelles, king boletes (also known as porcini or cèpes), morels, and matsutakes. But because other varieties do show up in Northwest farmers markets and other specialty outlets, this book addresses other species such as hedgehogs, lobsters, oysters, cauliflowers, and candy cap mushrooms, not to mention the celebrated American cousins of the European truffle, both black and white.

Foraging wild mushrooms is something like Easter egg hunting, if the eggs were painted grass-green and hidden deep in a thick lawn. Mushrooms seem to have innate camouflage, so beautifully suited to their environment that it takes a well-practiced eye to spot the mycological gems among the varied flora of the forest floor.

A greater skill yet is identifying the mushroom once found: knowledge of the different varieties, their habitat, and their edibility—which in mycology-speak ranges from "choice edible" (an understatement for delights such as king boletes and morels) to "unknown" to "deadly poisonous" (the latter referring to just a handful of species). I'm far from a mycology expert, though I do know enough to prefer the matsutake to the short-stemmed russula: they look rather alike, but it's night and day on the gastronomic side of things. In fact, the big "find" on my first foraging expedition was a trio of matsutakes and I felt like I'd won the lottery! Most of the foraging I do is at neighborhood farmers markets, at Seattle's Pike Place Market, and at other specialty shops that—thankfully—make easy work of bringing the diverse array of earthy, truly organic wild mushrooms into our kitchens.

The following pages are packed with information about Northwest wild mushrooms, plus forty recipes to make the most of that seasonal bounty.

The Northwest as Ideal Habitat

Wild," in its culinary sense, may nearly be relegated to the history books in another generation or two. The human race is working diligently to tame (or at least manage and control) everything in our path, including our food supply. Today there's little in our grocery stores that isn't essentially the product of human insistence.

One holdout, thankfully, is the world of wild mushrooms. Their biological makeup and quasi-mysterious life cycles have—for the most part—defied human intervention. The habitat in which many wild mushrooms thrive is quite elaborate. Some types rely on cohabitation with rootlets of specific trees, others thrive in the complex biomatter of decaying leaves and wood, still others flourish in the distinct mineral-rich parched landscape the year after a forest fire. While some "wild" mushrooms have been cultivated successfully for years (a thousand years or more, in the case of Asia's beloved shiitake mushroom), by far the greatest array of mushrooms is still to be found in the wild.

Lucky for those of us who call the Northwest home, the conditions in this region prove ideal for hundreds of mushroom varieties. Moisture is a crucial element in the growth of wild mushrooms and our abundant rainfall contributes immeasurably to the region's wealth of supply. In fact, most of our premier mushrooms show up in the fall only after the first substantial rainfall of the season. Another key reason that wild mushrooms are so abundant here is the great diversity of tree species—from Douglas fir to cottonwood to hazelnut—whose root systems serve as fertile habitat for the fungi. That combination of rain and trees—two of the most iconic characteristics of the Northwest—proves a rich foundation for our regional bounty of wild mushrooms.

Jack Czarnecki knows a thing or twelve about wild mushrooms. He grew up in a mycophile family of Polish descent and has been mushrooming most of his life. Before moving out to Oregon's Willamette Valley (prime mushrooming territory) in 1997, he cooked at his family's celebrated Joe's Restaurant in Reading, Pennsylvania, for many years. Czarnecki is now chef/owner of the Joel Palmer House in Dayton, Oregon, the restaurant's menu highlighting wild mushrooms to a degree that few others do. As he explained the moisture-mushroom relationship to me, in the eastern United States where rainfall is less consistent and more seasonal, mushrooms need a serious soaking rain to establish a growing spurt, then a follow-up "kicker" rain to bring up the fruit. Here in the Northwest, however, because our ground is typically more consistently moist, a small amount of rain can launch a mycelium into action. "All you have to do is spit on the ground and mushrooms will come up," jokes Czarnecki. So it can seem a nearly instantaneous change, one day no visible mushrooms, the next a bountiful supply ready for the picking.

Europe, particularly eastern Europe, counts expertise in wild mushroom harvest and cooking part of its culinary heritage. The arrival of these populations to the Northwest helped spark the recognition of the region's bounteous supply of wild mushrooms, free for the picking. Still today, this cultural affinity for wild mushrooms shows itself in the foragers of Czech, Polish, Hungarian, and other Eastern European roots, Veronica Williams on Washington's Long Beach Peninsula being one shining example (see page 38).

Mushroom Foraging—CAUTION: This book is not intended in any way to serve as a handbook for wild mushroom foraging. The art and science of hunting mushrooms is elaborate and it takes a good deal of education and field experience to safely collect edible wild mushrooms. Take to heart this oft-repeated saying: "There are old mushroom hunters and there are bold mushroom hunters, but there are no old, bold mushroom hunters." Never eat a mushroom you've picked yourself that you aren't absolutely certain you can identify! Another important mushroom adage is "When in doubt, throw it out." If you want to learn more about the specifics of foraging for wild mushrooms, join your local mycological society (see page 92) and hang out with the experts.

Asian cultures, too, have a traditional appreciation for wild mushrooms. As waves of Asian emigrants crossed the Pacific Ocean to the Northwest in the late nineteenth and early twentieth centuries, they headed into the hills in search of culinary treasures. The Japanese, especially, were probably astonished to find a very close sibling to their prized matsutake mushroom, or pine mushroom, in the lower foothills of the Cascade Mountains.

A relative handful of locals throughout the past century made forays into area forests for their private stash of wild mushrooms, but with little fanfare. The truth is that the region's supply of mushrooms went largely overlooked for many generations. There is little evidence that Native populations considered them an important food source. One of the best resources in my office library is the decades-old (but somehow timeless) Time-Life series, *Foods of the World*, its volume on the Pacific Northwest released in 1970. The author, Dale Brown, extolled the virtues of the region's wild mushroom habitat while pointing out the irony of that time: a chef at an Oregon Coast resort was paying almost $20 a pound (imagine today's adjustment for inflation) for dried morels from Europe when Brown wondered if "the same mushrooms could not have been picked fresh in the mountain forests behind his restaurant." How true!

It took the Northwest's gastronomic renaissance of the 1980s, with its flourishes of culinary enlightenment and attention to fresh regional ingredients, to address the wealth of wild mushrooms in our own backyard. Now, not only is this bounty far more appreciated by our region's chefs and home cooks—the idea of foraging a rediscovered old-world skill—but some of the harvest now travels to Japan and Europe, exported to the homelands of wild mushroom culture that first helped us value our native supply of these fungal treasures.

How Mushrooms Grow

It may seem a far-fetched association, but a wild mushroom can be compared to an apple. The mushroom is a fruiting body, like an apple, the means by which the organism assures continuation of its species. While apples carry seeds for propagation, mushrooms harbor countless thousands of microscopic spores. Where the analogy becomes more difficult is in understanding that the "tree" from which the mushrooms grow is a subterranean system called the mycelium. This feathery weblike structure can spread broadly underground and is the network from which the mushroom will fruit above ground at maturity (with the exception of truffles, which remain underground even when mature).

There are three basic systems of mushroom growth. Some of the key edible species we find in the Northwest (chanterelles, porcini, matsutakes, hedgehogs, among others) are mycorrhizal, meaning that they grow in a mutually beneficial relationship with a tree's root system (*myco* = mushroom, *rhiza* = root). Some mushroom species are selective (Oregon white truffles grow exclusively with Douglas fir trees), while others can be found in association with a range of tree species. The roots provide nutrients (especially carbohydrates, a by-product of photosynthesis) to the mushrooms that, in turn, draw moisture into the ground along with mineral nutrients important to the tree's health.

Another type of mushroom growth is saprophytic, the fungi thriving on dead organic matter such as rotting wood, old leaves, and/or other decomposing matter that provides distinctive nutrients. Among our region's saprophytic mushrooms are oyster mushrooms, shaggy manes, morels, and chicken of the woods.

Finally, some mushrooms live a parasitic life, drawing sustenance from their hosts and essentially killing them over time. One unusual instance of this is a mushroom that actually feeds off another one, the two together becoming what is known as the lobster mushroom, so named because of its often vivid orange hue that the interloping mushroom forms on the surface of its snow-white host. The cauliflower mushroom, too, relies on dead plant material, though sometimes it will create decay in living trees from which it can feed.

Exactly where and when wild mushrooms will be ripe for the picking—particularly the choice delectable varieties—is the big question. And there is no easy answer. Elevation, precipitation, temperature, and countless other elements—both natural and imposed—will affect the location and productivity of any mushroom patch.

Thousands of people in the Northwest make a living (or a partial one) from selling the wild mushrooms they collect. Many more recreational foragers preserve the secret location of "their spot" with profound determination. Master mycologist David Arora (author of *Mushrooms Demystified* and *All That the Rain Promises, and More . . .*) told a group of us at a foray during the Mendocino Wine and Mushroom Fest of a conversation he had with an Italian gentleman about foraging porcini. "When do porcini start coming up?" Arora asked the man. "Three weeks after the first inch of rain," the Italian responded matter-of-factly. "When do *you* start looking for porcini?" Arora persisted. "Ten days after the first inch of rain." It's a simple truth: the last one to the mushroom patch is generally left with slim pickings. Devotees typically divulge little about their mushrooming destinations.

One exception to this rule of secrecy is regional mycological societies, which devote themselves to education about wild mushrooms and supporting the more communal benefits of sharing expertise and mushroom-hunting labor. Organized forays that they plan for members are an outstanding way to learn more about wild mushrooms in your area. Even better, someone usually brings along a camp stove and everyone convenes at a nearby campsite to cook up some of the day's harvest for an incredible post-foray treat before heading home.

Our Regional Varieties

Chanterelles, golden or yellow *(Cantharellus cibarius)* and white *(C. subalbidus)*, are generally available summer and fall, sometimes even into winter depending on temperature and precipitation levels year to year. Golden is the more common of the two and is one of the most abundant of the edible wild mushrooms in the Northwest. Though annual harvest figures are difficult to pin down, it has been reported that as much as a million pounds of chanterelles can be harvested in the region in a year.

Chanterelles cook up with a moderate flavor that's earthy with a subtle fruitiness. They are versatile in the kitchen, particularly suited to sautéing. Chanterelles become quite tender when cooked, so I tend to cook them in larger pieces than I do other mushrooms, sometimes simply halved or quartered (even whole, if small). Sometimes available dried, an alternative for preserving them is canning or pickling. Kaspar Donier, chef/owner of Kaspar's restaurant in Seattle, is a fan of pickling chanterelles (and other mushrooms), which he collects around his farm near Mount Baker in northwestern Washington. Of Swiss descent, Kaspar has a lifelong love of mushrooms. Others sauté a season's bounty of chanterelles, then pack them in freezer bags for use during the coming months.

Black trumpets or black chanterelles *(Craterellus cornucopioides)*, also commonly known as horn of plenty, are equally delicious. Their texture is a bit firmer than that of the golden chanterelle, so they require a bit more cooking. Mendocino County, California, is a big producer of black trumpets in late winter/early spring; much of the harvest is exported to France where they're known by the dramatic but misleading name of *trompettes de la mort* (trumpets of death). Winter chanterelles *(Cantharellus infundibuliformis),* also known as yellow foot chanterelles, look only vaguely like their namesake, with a color that can range from dull yellow to medium brown. But the flavor and texture is similar, if milder, and they make a decent substitute later in the fall and winter season when other chanterelles are no longer available. Blue chanterelles *(Polyozellus multiplex)* are a less common but highly prized cousin. (I've witnessed a day's whole supply bought up— price no object—by one elated shopper at Sosio's in Seattle's Pike Place Market.) The color, when fresh, is a deep violet-blue, nearly black, hue that becomes distinctly ebony when cooked.

King bolete *(Boletus edulis),* also known by the French *cèpe* or Italian *porcini* (meaning "little pigs," a reflection of the mushroom's corpulence, especially its stem), is among the most prized wild mushrooms in the Northwest, north in Alaska, and indeed around the world. Lower elevations can produce king boletes fall to spring, depending on the depth of winter temperatures, and late spring to summer at higher elevations. This mushroom dries well, making it a good year-round option for recipes. Though stems are sometimes discarded from other mushrooms, not so with the king bolete, whose fat, meaty stem is as delectable as the cap.

The matsutake *(Tricholoma magnivelare)*

is a mushroom for which we look across the Pacific, rather than to Europe, for culinary inspiration. The matsutake, or pine mushroom, has been one of the most heralded culinary treasures in Japan for centuries (their native variety is the *T. matsutake*). As their own production of matsutake has waned in recent years, due to insects and disease as well as destruction of native habitat, Japanese buyers rely more and more on the Northwest, making it one of the most lucrative and scrutinized mushroom resources in the country.

The season for matsutake mushrooms begins in August in colder settings to the north, continues down the coast as fall establishes itself, and persists into January some years in central California, though they are most abundant in Washington and Oregon. The rather mundane-looking white mushroom is prized for its slightly spicy/peppery aroma and a firm texture that holds up well to all manner of cooking. It is at its best in simple recipes that allow the flavor of the mushroom to prevail.

Younger specimens of matsutake are most esteemed, when the cap is quite small and a fine veil hides the still-immature gilled underside of the cap. The mushrooms at this stage have yet to break through the forest undergrowth, requiring especially expert eyes to pinpoint the oh-so-subtle mounds of dirt formed by the caps. Larger, mature matsutakes are still tasty, but the distinctive flavor and aroma of the matsutake is most pronounced in the prized young mushrooms, many of which are sent to Japan.

Morels (*Morchella elata, M. angusticeps,* and *M. esculenta,* among others) are some of the most celebrated of the Northwest and Alaskan wild mushrooms, perhaps in part because they show up in late April or early May whereas most mushrooms fruit later in summer and fall. They'll fruit for only a few weeks, so get your fill while you can! Morels dry beautifully, making them a great candidate for year-round use, should you muster enough self-control to not eat every morel you buy during their peak season.

There are a few species of what are known as "true morels" common in the Northwest, each showing a range of size, form, color, etc. The distinguishing characteristics of the different species can be hard to decipher, so they are often expressed as one common group. The black morel (*M. elata),* however, is the predominant species, with a creamy white stem and knobby, pitted cap in a range of colors from soft brown to darker black-brown, often looking so much like a fallen pine cone as to be unnoticed by the scanning eye.

A mushroom that appears even earlier than the morel is *Verpa bohemica,* commonly called the "early morel," and though it looks vaguely like the true morel, it is not such a close relation. While the true morel has a hollow stem to which the pitted cap is completely attached (when halved, it looks as though the stem simply becomes the cap), the cap of the verpa is attached to the stem only at the very top, the cap flowing down around the stem like a skirt. These are also edible, but not as flavorful as true morels, so they are simply a preseason alternative while patiently waiting for the true morels to appear. Some tricky merchants may sell verpas as "morels" without distinguishing them from true morels. Check the caps to know for sure, as consumption of verpas in large quantities or over a series of days is not recommended.

Oyster mushrooms *(Pleurotus ostreatus)* are white to medium gray (or sometimes light brown), the cap often slightly elongated and gently fluted around the edge. There is little stem to these mushrooms, which grow not from the ground but out from the sides of trees, fallen logs, or stumps. Oysters have taken well to cultivation, and much of what we see in the grocery produce aisle was not collected in the wild. Cultivated oyster mushrooms may be available year-round, whereas wild specimens may be found only sporadically. You may have to hunt them down at specialty shops or farmers markets. If wild is what you have in mind, ask before you buy. The oyster is a versatile mushroom that's best in recipes that don't overpower its delicate flavor. A close relative is the angel wing mushroom *(Pleurocybella porrigens)*, whiter than the oyster and a bit milder in flavor, though not nearly as common in retail outlets.

The hedgehog mushroom *(Hydnum repandum)* is distinctive on the underside of the cap, which features tiny teeth or spines (thus the hedgehog reference) rather than the gills found on many other mushrooms. Pale gold-orange in color, hedgehogs are somewhat similar to chanterelles in flavor and texture and can be used interchangeably with them. This is also a fall variety, though they hold up longer than chanterelles and continue to fruit through the winter in some of the milder coastal areas.

One of the most otherworldly looking of the Northwest wild mushrooms is the cauliflower mushroom *(Sparassis crispa)*, which grows in large rounded forms off-white to pale yellow in color with deeply fluted ribs, looking somewhat brainlike. The flesh is quite firm, some say tough, but thorough cooking makes it tender, still with a slightly crisp bite that's in nice contrast to the softer texture of many mushrooms. They hold up well to long cooking, making a good candidate for soups, stews, and baked dishes (such as potato gratin). Because of their convoluted ribbonlike formation, you need to take extra care in cleaning cauliflower mushrooms. It's best to cut them into smaller pieces and brush away any needles, dirt, or other debris that's lodged inside.

The lobster mushroom *(Hypomyces lactifluorum)* is interesting because you actually get two mushrooms in one. The mushroom of note is simply the visible outer surface, commonly a vivid orange color (hence "lobster"), parasitizing another mushroom that lies just under the surface. The host is generally the short-stemmed russula *(Russula brevipes)*, which while abundant in our region is one of the least interesting mushrooms out there, edible but not really worth stooping over to pick up. It's interesting that the synergy between the two types of mushrooms produces such different flavor and texture in the host. The meaty, firm texture of the lobster mushroom makes it a good choice for grilling or roasting.

Ah, the truffle. Right up there with caviar

and Champagne, this knobby, dirty-looking underground mushroom is one of the most highly touted foods in the world. Did you think they only came from the Périgord region of France and the Piedmont region of Italy? Think again. Think Oregon. The Oregon white truffle *(Tuber gibbosum)* is found from British Columbia to central California, but is most prolific in Oregon. Likewise, the Oregon black truffle *(Leucangium carthusiana)* is most abundant in that state, though more a second cousin than a sibling of the true European black truffle *(Tuber melanosporum)*. Debate rages about the status of the Oregon truffles, some finding both white and black varieties to be

on par with the traditionally celebrated French and Italian ones, others finding them mere shadows of their European counterparts. For more on Northwest truffles, see page 84.

There are many other delicious wild mushrooms found in the Northwest—including chicken of the woods *(Laetiporus sulphureus)*, honey mushrooms *(Armillaria mellea)*, shaggy manes *(Coprinus comatus)*, lion's manes *(Hericium erinaceus)*, puffballs *(Calvatia gigantea* and others), hawk's wings *(Sarcodon imbricatum)*—though most of these are available only to the forager and, on occasion, in farmers markets or other limited outlets.

About the Recipes

True of many of the Northwest's most celebrated regional foods, there is a seasonal, and rather unpredictable, rhythm to wild mushrooms. From year to year and month to month, the supply of wild mushrooms can be irregular. Most of the recipes in this book simply call for "wild mushrooms" rather than specific varieties, so that the recipes are as versatile as possible: you may just as well use hedgehog mushrooms once the season's chanterelles have come and gone. If wild mushrooms aren't widely available in your area, see the resource guide (page 92) for some Northwest companies that offer mail-order service for fresh wild mushrooms. Certainly, feel free to use cultivated mushrooms in place of wild when the latter aren't available. In some recipes, a tasty compromise is to use dried wild mushrooms,

though often it's best to use fresh cultivated mushrooms as well to provide bulk while the dried mushrooms offer distinctive flavor.

Most of the recipes call for mushrooms by weight rather than volume, as it is a much more consistent and reliable means for measurement, particularly since mushrooms are too bulky to measure by the cup unless they are well chopped. You may simply purchase the amount needed, using the scale at the store, though I find I get quite a lot of use out of my digital kitchen scale.

When it comes to cooking with wild mushrooms, it's important to note that even some highly prized wild mushrooms contain mild toxins that can be harmful to some people but are eliminated in cooking. To be safe, wild mushrooms should always be fully cooked before eating them.

Breakfast / Brunch

Baked Eggs with Wild Mushrooms and Caramelized Onions

A simple and savory way to start the day, this dish uses a nest of wild mushrooms and caramelized onions in which to bake individual eggs. To save time in the morning, you could prepare the caramelized onion-mushroom mixture the night before and refrigerate, covered.

2 tablespoons vegetable oil	Salt and freshly ground black pepper
1 large onion, thinly sliced	4 eggs
¾ pound wild mushrooms, brushed clean, trimmed, and thinly sliced	¼ cup crème fraîche or whipping cream
	Toast, for serving

Preheat the oven to 400°F. Generously butter four 4-ounce ramekins or other small baking dishes.

Heat the oil in a large skillet over medium heat. Add the onion and sauté gently, stirring occasionally, until the onion is quite tender and just beginning to brown, about 10 minutes. Add the mushrooms and cook until the onion is nicely caramelized and the mushrooms are tender and any liquid they give off has evaporated, stirring often, 20 to 25 minutes longer. Season to taste with salt and pepper.

Spoon the onion-mushroom mixture into the prepared ramekins, drawing up the edges slightly to make a nest for the egg. Break an egg into each ramekin and spoon 1 tablespoon of the cream over each egg, then season the tops lightly with salt and pepper. Put the ramekins in a baking dish, pour boiling water into the dish to come about halfway up the sides of the ramekins, and bake until the egg whites are set and the yolks are still soft, about 15 minutes. Carefully lift the ramekins from the water and dry off the bottoms of the dishes, then set them on individual plates. Serve right away, with toast alongside.

Makes 4 servings

Wild Mushroom and Herb Strata

This recipe can be assembled and refrigerated overnight, the strata baked just before serving the next morning. If doing so, take the dish from the refrigerator about 15 minutes before baking, so it can come close to room temperature before going into the hot oven. The recipe could also be doubled to bake in a 9-by-13-inch baking dish for a larger brunch.

3 tablespoons unsalted butter

1 pound wild mushrooms, brushed
   clean, trimmed, and sliced

½ cup sliced green onions

1 can (14 ounces) artichoke hearts,
   drained and rinsed

2 tablespoons minced chives

2 teaspoons minced tarragon

2 tablespoons minced flat-leaf
   (Italian) parsley

Salt and freshly ground black pepper

About 10 ounces sliced white bread
   (¾ of a medium loaf)

1½ cups grated Swiss cheese

6 eggs

2 cups half-and-half

Preheat the oven to 400°F. Generously butter a 9-inch square baking dish or other 2-quart baking dish.

Melt the butter in a large skillet over medium heat. Add the mushrooms and green onions and cook, stirring often, until the mushrooms are tender and any liquid they give off has evaporated, 8 to 10 minutes. Transfer the mushroom mixture to a large bowl and set aside. Thinly slice the artichoke hearts and add them to the mushrooms with the chives, parsley, and tarragon. Season to taste with salt and pepper, toss well, and set aside.

Trim the crusts from the bread and discard the heels (or save for another use). Cut the bread slices in half diagonally. Lay about half the pieces, slightly overlapping, in the bottom of the baking dish. Spoon the mushroom mixture over the bread and sprinkle with 1 cup of the Swiss cheese. Top with the remaining bread slices, slightly overlapping the triangles.

Whisk the eggs in a medium bowl just to break them up, then add the half-and-half with a good pinch each of salt and pepper. Continue whisking until frothy, another minute or so. Gradually pour the egg mixture evenly over the bread and mushroom layers, allowing it to slowly seep down among the ingredients. Sprinkle the remaining cheese over the top.

Bake until the egg is cooked through (a knife inserted in the center should come out clean) and the top is browned, about 1 hour. If the top is browned before the strata is cooked through, cover lightly with foil. Let sit for 10 minutes or so before cutting into pieces to serve.

Makes 6 servings

My Porcini Weekend

I had always imagined ideal wild mushroom territory to be the dense underbrush of old-growth forests at moderately high elevations. When I headed off to Washington's Long Beach Peninsula for the annual Wild Mushroom Festival, I really didn't know what to expect. It was a quick education about the diversity of mushroom habitats here in the

Northwest, to say the least, seeing outstanding mushrooms growing within a couple hundred yards of the roaring Pacific coastline. As it happens, I had dropped in on a healthy run of celebrated king bolete mushrooms (porcini) and would soon be eating my fill.

Staying at the historic Shelburne Inn in Seaview, we feasted the first night on an array of locally harvested wild mushrooms at a special festival dinner at the adjacent Shoalwater restaurant. The six-course menu featured lobster mushrooms, matsutakes, chanterelles, and delicious milk caps *(Lactarius deliciosus)*—but best among them were the roasted porcini served alongside a phyllo packet stuffed with a mix of wild mushrooms, the white wine sauce embellished with porcini as well. Mmm-mmm, this got the weekend off to a great start!

The next night's dinner at The Ark restaurant in nearby Nahcotta offered some irresistible specials. Continuing the theme, I opted for the grilled Alaska halibut and Pacific coho salmon served with big, meaty slices of pan-fried porcini, the earthy-nutty perfume of the mushrooms perfectly suited to the delicious fresh fish. Even breakfast at the Shelburne Inn was a porcini-lover's paradise, an embarrassment of the mushrooms sautéed up by chef/innkeeper David Campiche in his seasonal frittata. Oh, what a weekend.

It wasn't all about eating, though! As part of the festival activities, dozens of enthusiasts gathered with Veronica Williams (more about this dynamo-mycologist on page 38) in a nearby park to soak up some of her abundant enthusiasm for and knowledge of the region's wild mushrooms. Later that day, I took another impromptu foray with Campiche and we hit porcini pay dirt, the fat, broad-capped, medium brown mushrooms expertly hiding among fallen leaves, piles of pine needles, and moss. Such a thrill. Some of those specimens made it back home with me, and were cooked up for the Porcini Crostini (page 32) and the extra-special breakfast treat of Wild Mushroom Hash (page 28).

Boletus edulis

Candy Cap and Pecan Waffles

This distinctive recipe comes from Alan Kantor, chef at MacCallum House in Mendocino, California, one of the most mushroom-loving areas on the West Coast. After talking with Alan about the distinct aroma and flavor characteristics of candy cap mushrooms, he sent this really outstanding waffle recipe my way—a surprising way to serve up wild mushrooms at breakfast time, delicious with a drizzle of good maple syrup. There is a lot of nutty-toasty-earthy flavor in these waffles, thanks to the array of ingredients used. Amaranth seed is an ancient grain long grown in North America, highly nutritious and very crunchy. It is available in organic food stores and well-stocked grocery stores.

¼ ounce dried candy cap mushrooms
½ cup old-fashioned rolled oats
¼ cup amaranth seed
¼ cup currants or raisins
1 tablespoon molasses
3 tablespoons unsalted butter
¾ cup all-purpose flour
1½ teaspoons baking powder
½ teaspoon baking soda
¼ cup cornmeal
¼ cup buckwheat flour
¼ teaspoon salt
2 eggs
1 cup buttermilk
½ cup pecans, toasted and
   coarsely chopped

Put the candy cap mushrooms in a small bowl and cover with about 1 cup of boiling water. Set aside until softened and cool, about 30 minutes.

Combine the oats, amaranth, currants, and molasses with 1¼ cups cold water in a medium saucepan and bring just to a boil over medium-high heat. Reduce the heat to low and continue to simmer until the mixture is very thick and all the liquid is absorbed, stirring often, 8 to 10 minutes. Remove the saucepan from the heat and set aside.

Drain the mushrooms, reserving the soaking liquid. Squeeze excess water from the mushrooms and finely chop them. Slowly drizzle the reserved liquid into the oat mixture, being careful to leave behind any sediment in the bottom of the bowl. Melt the butter in a small saucepan over low heat and add the chopped mushrooms. Cook them just until soft, 3 to 5 minutes, and then stir the mushrooms and melted butter into the oat mixture.

Preheat a waffle iron.

Sift the all-purpose flour, baking powder, and baking soda into a large bowl. Stir in the cornmeal, buckwheat flour, and salt. In a separate bowl, use a fork to lightly beat together the eggs and buttermilk, then use a wooden spoon to stir the wet ingredients into the dry ingredients. Gently fold in the pecans and the oat mixture just until combined.

Lightly butter the waffle iron and pour in a generous ½ cup of the batter (more or less depending on the size of your iron). Close the waffle iron and cook until well browned and crisp, 5 to 7 minutes. Continue with the remaining batter, keeping the cooked waffles warm in a low oven.

Makes 6 servings

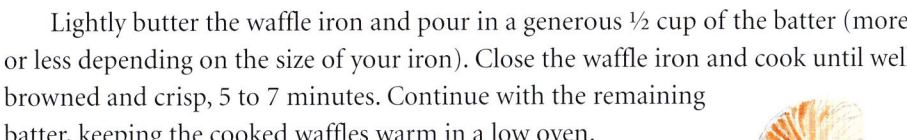

Scrambled Eggs with Wild Mushrooms and Goat Cheese

Simple scrambled eggs are one of my favorite choices for starting the day, and a versatile option too. In this dish, creamy, tangy goat cheese is a delicious complement to the eggs, with wild mushrooms adding their meaty-earthy character. Most any kind of wild mushroom may be used in this recipe, or use a mix of different mushroom varieties if you prefer.

2 tablespoons unsalted butter
6 to 8 ounces wild mushrooms, brushed clean, trimmed, and sliced
4 eggs

¼ cup milk
Salt and freshly ground black pepper
1 tablespoon minced chives
5 ounces fresh goat cheese, crumbled
2 English muffins

Melt the butter in a medium skillet over medium heat. Add the mushrooms and cook, stirring occasionally, until they are tender and any liquid they give off has evaporated, 5 to 7 minutes. While the mushrooms are cooking, whisk the eggs with the milk until frothy, and season with a good pinch of salt and pepper. Pour the eggs over the mushrooms and cook, stirring often, until the eggs are nearly set, about 5 minutes. Stir the chives into the eggs, then scatter the goat cheese over and stir to gently incorporate so that some of the cheese pieces remain intact while some melt creamily into the eggs. Taste for seasoning, adding more salt or pepper to taste.

Toast the English muffins and set them cut-side up on individual plates. Spoon the scrambled egg mixture over the muffins and serve right away.

Makes 2 servings

Candy Cap Butter Cookies

The small, deep orange candy cap mushrooms *(Lactarius fragilis)* seem of little note in their fresh state, but when dried (and to a lesser degree, when cooked fresh), they evoke an astonishingly sweet, aromatic character strongly reminiscent of maple syrup. I first ate candy caps in cookies baked by Alan Kantor of the MacCallum House restaurant in Mendocino, the recipe attributed to David Arora's book *All That the Rain Promises, and More . . . .* My version of the cookie is below, ideal to serve with a simple ice cream sundae for a dinner party dessert. Kantor's recipe for candy cap waffles is on page 22.

¼ ounce dried candy cap mushrooms,
 crumbled
2 cups all-purpose flour
1 cup unsalted butter, at room temperature

1½ cups powdered sugar
1 egg
½ teaspoon salt

Combine the candy cap mushrooms with ¼ cup of the flour in a food processor and pulse to finely mince the mushrooms; set aside.

Cream the butter and sugar in an electric mixture at medium speed until well blended and fluffy. Add the egg and continue mixing until it is well incorporated. Mix in the salt and reduce the speed to low. Add the candy cap/flour mixture, then begin gradually adding the remaining flour, scraping down the sides of the bowl as needed, until the dough is evenly blended.

Cut a piece of waxed paper or plastic wrap about 2 feet long. Spoon the cookie dough down the length of the paper and form it into a log about 1½ inches across. Wrap the dough securely in the paper, twisting the ends to form a solid cylinder. Refrigerate the dough for at least 1 hour before baking.

Preheat the oven to 375°F. Lightly grease a heavy baking sheet.

Unwrap the dough and cut it across into slices about ¼ inch thick. Arrange the rounds on the baking sheet with at least 1 inch between them. Bake until firm and lightly browned around the edges, about 12 minutes. Transfer the cookies to a wire rack to cool while baking the remaining cookies.

Makes about 5 dozen cookies

Poached Eggs with Morels and Spinach

From The Aerie Resort on Vancouver Island, British Columbia, comes this delightful and elegant twist on the morning egg. Chef Christophe Letard is adamant about making the most of regional products—from asparagus to venison to berries—which visitors enjoy in the resort's dining room. In the fall, guests can even sign up for mushroom foraging trips with the chef and a local mushroom expert (see page 90).

This dish is a bit more sophisticated when served at The Aerie, where they finish it with a drizzle of red wine reduction. They also top the eggs with a hazelnut tuile, an elaborate flourish befitting the stylish resort, but the poached eggs are delicious as is, with freshly buttered toast and/or potatoes alongside.

2 tablespoons olive oil
2 ounces morel mushrooms, brushed
   clean, trimmed, and sliced
1 shallot, finely chopped
1 small bunch spinach
   (about 8 ounces),
   rinsed, dried, and tough
   stems removed
Salt and freshly ground black pepper
2 tablespoons unsalted butter
2 tablespoons distilled white vinegar
2 eggs

Heat the olive oil in a large skillet over medium heat. Add the morels and shallot and sauté, stirring occasionally, until the morels are tender, 3 to 5 minutes. Add the spinach leaves, a handful at a time, stirring to wilt each batch before adding more. When all of the spinach is wilted and tender, drain off any accumulated liquid from the skillet, season to taste with salt and pepper, and stir in the butter to evenly mix. Set aside over very low heat while poaching the eggs.

Half-fill a deep skillet with water and add the vinegar. Bring the water to a gentle boil over medium-high heat, then carefully crack the eggs into the water. (To avoid scalding your knuckles, you could first crack each egg into a small bowl, then gently tip the egg from the bowl into the water.) Reduce the heat to medium and simmer gently until the egg whites are set and the yolks are still soft, 3 to 4 minutes, gently sloshing some of the water over the top of the eggs with a spoon once or twice during cooking to help set the surface of the yolk. Scoop out the eggs with a slotted spoon and drain them on a plate lined with paper towels.

Spoon the spinach-morel mixture into the center of individual plates, set a poached egg on top, and serve right away.

Makes 2 servings

Savory Wild Mushroom Shortcake

This recipe is a Northwest variation on that Southern breakfast staple of biscuits and gravy. The rich creamy gravy still starts with crumbled sausage but is embellished with a good dose of wild mushrooms, the rich combo served atop tender biscuits that are speckled with minced chive. A hearty breakfast to be sure.

½ pound bulk pork sausage meat
¾ pound wild mushrooms, brushed
    clean, trimmed, and coarsely chopped
¼ cup minced onion

¼ cup all-purpose flour
2 cups milk or half-and-half
2 tablespoons minced chives
Salt and freshly ground black pepper

Biscuits

2 cups all-purpose flour
1 tablespoon baking powder
½ teaspoon salt

6 tablespoons unsalted butter,
    cut into pieces and chilled
¾ cup milk
2 tablespoons minced chives

Preheat the oven to 400°F. Lightly butter a heavy baking sheet.

For the biscuits, combine the flour, baking powder, and salt in a food processor and pulse once or twice to blend. Add the butter and pulse until it is finely chopped and the mixture has the texture of coarse cornmeal. (Alternatively, cut the butter into the flour using a pastry cutter or two table knives.) Transfer the mixture to a bowl, add the milk and chives, and gently stir until the batter is evenly mixed; avoid overmixing or the biscuits won't be as light as they could be.

Transfer the biscuit dough to a lightly floured work surface. Press the dough into a circle about 6 inches across and 1 inch thick. Cut the dough into quarters, setting the biscuits on the baking sheet with at least 1 inch between them. Bake until the biscuits are puffed and lightly browned on top, 12 to 15 minutes. Transfer the biscuits to a wire rack to cool.

Cook the sausage in a large skillet over medium heat until cooked through and lightly browned, 12 to 15 minutes, stirring often and breaking up the sausage chunks as they cook. If there is more than about 2 tablespoons of fat in the skillet, spoon out and discard the excess. Add the mushrooms and onion, increase the heat to medium-high, and cook, stirring occasionally, until the mushrooms are tender and any liquid they give off has evaporated, 5 to 7 minutes. Add the flour and cook for 1 to 2 minutes longer, stirring so that the flour evenly coats the sausage and mushrooms. Slowly stir in the milk and cook until the gravy has thickened, 5 to 7 minutes. Stir in the chives and season to taste with salt and pepper.

To serve, cut each of the biscuits in half horizontally and set the bottom halves on individual plates. Generously spoon the mushroom-sausage gravy over, top with the biscuit tops, and serve right away.

Makes 4 servings

Wild Mushroom Hash

This hearty hash is a perfect accompaniment to your favorite eggs, whether simply scrambled or in a fancy omelet. It also serves as an ideal warm perch for poached eggs. Or even consider it as a dinnertime side dish for roasted chicken or grilled steaks.

3 tablespoons unsalted butter
1 pound new potatoes, scrubbed and
    cut into ½-inch dice
½ cup finely chopped onion
Salt and freshly ground
    black pepper

1 pound wild mushrooms,
    brushed clean, trimmed, and
    coarsely chopped
¼ cup chopped green onion
2 tablespoons minced flat-leaf
    (Italian) parsley

Melt the butter in a medium skillet, preferably nonstick, over medium-high heat. Add the potatoes and onion and cook, stirring, until the onion is tender and aromatic and the potatoes are starting to soften, 3 to 5 minutes. Season lightly with salt and pepper, then reduce the heat to medium and cook, stirring occasionally, until the potatoes are tender and partly browned, 8 to 10 minutes. Stir in the mushrooms and green onion and cook, stirring occasionally, until the mushrooms are tender and any liquid they give off has evaporated, about 15 minutes. Taste the hash for seasoning, adding more salt or pepper to taste. Stir in the parsley and serve right away.

Makes 4 servings

Appetizers

Wild Mushroom and Cabbage Strudel

Packaged phyllo dough is a godsend for a wide variety of recipes, making easy work of creating fancy, flaky treats, both savory and sweet. This strudel is one great example. A simple sauté of cabbage with its hint of sweetness is paired with tender wild mushrooms for the filling. The surprise is a bit of shredded tart apple, which distinctly complements the flavors.

Rather than making one large strudel, you may also make individual strudels, using 6 phyllo sheets (1 per serving) and forming them much like the larger one. I have recently found half-sized sheets of phyllo dough in stores that are ideal for individual-sized portions.

2 tablespoons olive oil
¾ pound wild mushrooms, brushed
  clean, trimmed, and sliced
½ large head napa cabbage
  (about 1½ pounds),
  cored and finely shredded
½ onion, thinly sliced
½ cup dry white wine

1 tart apple, cored, peeled,
  and finely grated
2 tablespoons minced flat-leaf
  (Italian) parsley
1 teaspoon minced dill
Salt and freshly ground white
  or black pepper
8 sheets phyllo dough
½ cup unsalted butter, melted

Dill Beurre Blanc

6 tablespoons dry white wine
1 tablespoon white wine vinegar
1 shallot, minced

1 cup unsalted butter, cut into pieces
  and chilled
1½ teaspoons minced dill

Heat the olive oil in a large skillet over medium-high heat. Add the mushrooms and sauté, stirring often, until they begin to brown around the edges and give off some of their liquid, 3 to 4 minutes. Add the cabbage and onion and cook, stirring, until the cabbage just begins to wilt, 1 to 2 minutes. Add the wine, stir, and continue to cook until the vegetables are tender and all of the liquid has evaporated, 10 to 12 minutes, stirring occasionally. Take the skillet from the heat and stir in the apple, parsley, and dill with salt and pepper to taste. Transfer to a medium bowl and set aside to cool completely.

Preheat the oven to 375°F.

Lay one of the phyllo dough sheets lengthwise on the counter and lightly brush melted butter over the surface. Top with another dough sheet, matching up the edges, and brush it with butter. Continue layering with the remaining dough sheets, lightly brushing the top one as well.

If any liquid has accumulated in the filling, drain it off so that the strudel won't be soggy. Spoon the cooled mushroom filling onto the phyllo, spreading it out evenly up to three of the edges, leaving a 1-inch border along the long edge closest to you. Lightly brush the exposed dough strip with a little more melted butter. Beginning at the long edge farthest away from you, roll the phyllo sheets toward you, ending with the seam underneath.

Carefully transfer the strudel roll to a baking sheet and brush the surface with a bit more melted butter. Bake the strudel until the dough is nicely browned, about 45 minutes.

While the strudel is baking, make the dill beurre blanc. Combine the wine, vinegar, and shallot in a small heavy saucepan and bring to a boil over high heat. Reduce the heat to medium-high and continue to boil until there is only about 1 tablespoon of liquid remaining, 3 to 5 minutes. Reduce the heat to low and begin adding the butter in pieces, constantly whisking between each addition so the cold butter melts slowly and creates a creamy sauce. Take the pan off the heat as needed to avoid overheating the sauce, which will cause the butter to "break" and the sauce to become oily. When all the butter has been added, whisk in the dill and season to taste with salt and pepper. Keep the sauce warm over very low heat until ready to serve.

Transfer the strudel carefully to a cutting board and cut across into 12 rounds about 1 inch thick. Arrange 2 or 3 rounds on each plate, drizzle some of the dill beurre blanc over and around the strudel, and serve right away.

Makes 4 to 6 servings

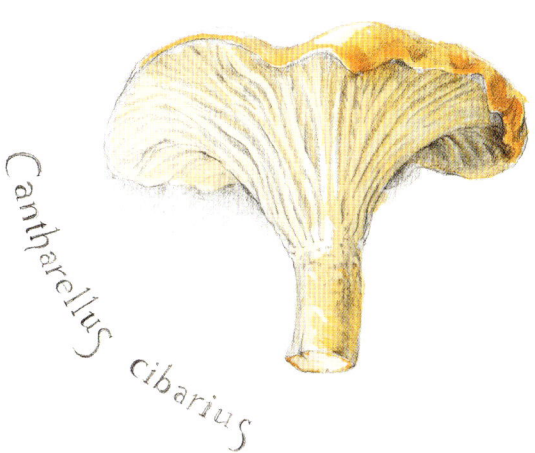

Cantharellus cibarius

Porcini Crostini

Inspired by a conversation with master mushroomer Veronica Williams (page 38), this recipe proves that simple can be sublime, showing off prized fresh porcini to great effect. This wouldn't be a good recipe for using dried mushrooms; if fresh porcini aren't available, use whatever fresh wild mushrooms are available, or a mix of different varieties. Mellow fresh herbs, such as chervil or flat-leaf (Italian) parsley, would be delicious additions if you choose. There's no more elegant a nibble to have with a glass of Champagne or a cocktail before dinner.

1 baguette, preferably hearty artisan-style
4 tablespoons olive oil

8 to 10 ounces porcini, brushed clean, trimmed, and very finely chopped
2 cloves garlic, minced
Salt and freshly ground black pepper

Preheat the oven to 450°F.

Cut the baguette into ½ inch slices on the bias, discarding the ends; you should have about 24 slices. Arrange the slices in a single layer on a baking sheet and toast in the oven until good and crisp and lightly browned, 5 to 7 minutes. Take the pan from the oven and brush the tops lightly with about half of the olive oil; set aside.

Heat the remaining 2 tablespoons of the olive oil in a medium skillet over medium-high heat. Add the porcini and garlic and cook, stirring often, until the mushrooms are tender and any liquid they give off has evaporated, 3 to 5 minutes. Season to taste with salt and pepper.

Spoon a scant tablespoon of the warm porcini mixture onto each of the toasted bread slices, arrange them on a platter, and serve right away.

Makes 6 to 8 servings

Wild Mushroom Tempura

For the most dazzling presentation, use a variety of mushrooms of different shapes and textures, such as chanterelles, oyster mushrooms, porcini, cauliflower mushrooms, morels—a wide range is well suited to this recipe. Also feel free to add other ingredients—such as onion, shrimp, strips of fish, zucchini slices, or asparagus—to accompany the mushrooms. There is easily enough tempura batter to accommodate such additions.

This thin batter fries up light and allows you to see the mushrooms and other items beneath the crisp batter veil. It won't coat the foods as generously as beer batter might.

1 to 1½ pounds mixed wild
   mushrooms, brushed clean

1 bunch green onions, trimmed
Vegetable oil, for deep-frying

Dipping Sauce

⅓ cup mirin (sweet rice wine) or sake
¼ cup soy sauce
¼ cup dashi, vegetable broth, or water

1 tablespoon finely grated daikon
   (white radish)
1 teaspoon grated ginger

Tempura Batter

1 egg
1 cup ice water, more if needed

1 cup rice flour or all-purpose flour

For the dipping sauce, combine the mirin, soy sauce, dashi, daikon, and ginger in a small saucepan and bring just to a simmer. Take from the heat and let cool. The sauce may be made 1 to 2 days in advance and refrigerated, but let the sauce come to room temperature before serving.

Trim any tough stems from the mushrooms. Cut the mushrooms into pieces no more than ½ inch thick. For cauliflower mushrooms, simply trim into smaller clusters. Morels can be fried whole, though if quite large you should halve them. Cut the green onions in half crosswise.

Heat about 3 inches of the oil in a large, heavy saucepan (the oil should not come more than halfway up the sides of the pan) over medium-high heat to about 375°F.

When the oil is hot, make the batter. Beat the egg with a fork in a medium bowl, then beat in the ice water. Add the flour gradually, beating gently as you go. You want to mix the batter only lightly to avoid making it stiff. It should be thin enough to just delicately coat the vegetables. If it's a bit too thick, beat in another tablespoon or two of ice water.

Working with 5 or 6 mushroom pieces at a time, drop them into the batter and lift them out one by one with the fork, allowing excess batter to drip off. Gently add the coated mushrooms to the hot oil and fry until crisp and lightly browned, 2 to 3 minutes. Scoop them out with a slotted spoon and drain on paper towels. Keep the fried mushrooms warm in a low oven while frying the rest. Stir the batter gently between batches, especially if using rice flour, which quickly settles in the bowl. Fry the green onion pieces in the same way.

Stir the dipping sauce to mix and pour it into separate bowls. Arrange the mushrooms and green onions on individual plates, setting the dipping sauce alongside, and serve right away.

Makes 4 servings

Buckwheat Crêpes with Wild Mushrooms, Ham, and Gruyère

The buckwheat crêpe reigns supreme in Brittany in Northwest France. A highlight of a visit to that region is a dinner of these nutty-tasting, savory crêpes filled with a simple composition of ingredients: ham and cheese, or tomato and mushroom, or smoked salmon with crème fraîche. This recipe is a variation on the classic ham-and-cheese combination, embellished with sautéed wild mushrooms. In France, "crêpe" typically refers only to the simpler all-purpose-flour type used for sweet recipes, while this buckwheat version is called a "galette." If you don't have long chives available for tying together the crêpe packets, you may instead simply fold the crêpe—first in from the sides, then down from the top and up from the bottom. Then flip the squarish packet over so that the seam is underneath for serving.

2 tablespoons olive oil
½ cup minced onion
¾ pound mixed wild mushrooms, brushed clean, trimmed, and coarsely chopped

1 tablespoon minced flat-leaf (Italian) parsley
4 ounces thinly sliced ham
4 ounces Gruyère cheese, thinly sliced
6 long chives (optional)

Buckwheat Crêpes

¾ cup all-purpose flour
¾ cup buckwheat flour
¾ teaspoon salt
1½ cups milk
1 cup water

2 eggs, lightly beaten
2 tablespoons unsalted butter, melted and cooled, plus more for cooking the crêpes

Tomato Sauce

3 tablespoons olive oil
1 onion, coarsely chopped
3 cloves garlic, chopped
2 teaspoons minced thyme
½ teaspoon minced oregano
1 bay leaf

1 can (14 ounces) whole or chopped tomatoes
¾ cup water
¼ cup tomato paste
Salt and freshly ground black pepper

For the crêpes, combine the all-purpose and buckwheat flours and the salt in a medium bowl. Stir with a fork to mix, then make a well in the center. Add the milk, water, and eggs to the well in the flour and stir with the fork for about 1 minute to fully blend. Stir in the melted butter. Cover the bowl and refrigerate for 1 to 2 hours before cooking.

While the crêpe batter is resting, make the tomato sauce. Heat the olive oil in a medium saucepan over medium heat. Add the onion and garlic and cook, stirring, until tender and aromatic, 3 to 5 minutes. Stir in the thyme, oregano, and bay leaf. Add the tomatoes and their liquid with the water and tomato paste. Stir to mix, then lower the heat and simmer the sauce partly covered until the sauce is slightly thickened and the flavors are nicely melded, 30 to 40 minutes, stirring occasionally. Let cool slightly and remove the bay leaf. Purée the sauce with an immersion blender or in a food processor or blender. Return the sauce to the pan and season to taste with salt and pepper; set aside.

Lightly coat a 10-inch crêpe pan or skillet with melted butter and heat it over medium heat. Stir the crêpe batter once again to remix after sitting. Add ¼ cup of the batter to the pan and quickly but gently swirl the pan so the batter evenly coats the base. Cook the crêpe until the surface turns from shiny to dull and the edges are just beginning to curl, 30 to 60 seconds. Using a small spatula, carefully flip it and cook on the other side until lightly browned on the bottom, about 1 minute longer. Transfer the crêpe to a plate and continue with the remaining crêpes, stacking them one on top of the other. It's very common for the first (and sometimes second) crêpe to be a total failure, so don't think twice about tossing out early crêpes that don't work. You want a total of 6 good crêpes for this dish.

Preheat the oven to 350°F. Line a baking sheet with a piece of lightly oiled parchment paper or foil.

Heat the oil in a medium skillet over medium-high heat. Add the onion and cook, stirring, until tender and aromatic, 2 to 3 minutes. Add the mushrooms and cook, stirring occasionally, until tender and any liquid they give off has evaporated, 5 to 7 minutes. Take the pan from the heat and stir in the parsley, with salt and pepper to taste.

Set one of the crêpes on the work surface with the more attractive side down. Lay some of the ham in the center of the crêpe (the ham should come to within no less than 2 inches of the edge of the crêpe; trim and/or overlap if necessary). Top the ham with slices of Gruyère. Spoon a mound of mushrooms in the center, then draw the crêpe up around the mushrooms and tie the top together with a chive. Set the crêpe on the baking sheet and continue with the remaining ingredients, making a total of 6 packets.

Heat the crêpes in the oven just until warmed through so that the cheese melts, about 10 minutes. Also reheat the tomato sauce over medium heat. To serve, spoon the tomato sauce onto individual plates, top each with a crêpe, and serve right away.

Makes 6 servings

Truffled Deviled Eggs

The recent retro/comfort food trend has brought timeless classics, like the deviled egg, back into our lives. This snack is one of my all-time favorites, made luxurious with the addition of minced Oregon white truffle. The rich but mellow flavor of the hard-cooked egg yolk is a great vehicle for making the most of the truffle's distinctive aroma and flavor. If you have truffle oil on hand, a few drops added to the filling will enhance the truffleness of the dish. Fancy cocktail fare, to be sure!

6 eggs	1 teaspoon minced shallot or onion
¼ cup mayonnaise	1 teaspoon minced chives
2 to 3 teaspoons minced white truffle	Salt and freshly ground white pepper

Put the eggs in a pan with enough cold water to cover them by about 1 inch. Put the pan over high heat and bring to a boil, then reduce the heat to medium-high and set the timer for 10 minutes. Drain the eggs and run cold water over them for a few minutes to stop the cooking and help cool the eggs quickly (which helps make them easier to peel).

Peel the eggs and cut each in half lengthwise. Scoop the egg yolks into a small bowl, setting the whites on a plate. Mash the egg yolks with a fork, then add the mayonnaise and continue mashing until smooth. Stir in the truffle, shallot, and half of the chives with salt and pepper to taste.

Spoon the filling into the egg white cavities. For a fancier finish, you could instead fill the eggs using a pastry bag fitted with a large star tip. Sprinkle the remaining chives over the egg yolk filling and serve.

Makes 4 to 6 servings

Homemade Mayonnaise

1 egg yolk
2 teaspoons white wine vinegar
¾ cup olive oil (not extra virgin)
Salt and freshly ground white pepper

In a medium bowl, combine the egg yolk with the vinegar and whisk to blend. Begin adding the olive oil a few drops at a time, whisking constantly, until the yolk begins to turn pale and thicken slightly, showing that an emulsion has begun to form. Continue adding the rest of the oil in a thin, steady stream, whisking constantly. Season to taste with salt and pepper.

Alternatively, combine the egg yolk and vinegar in a food processor and pulse to blend. With the blades running, begin adding the oil a few drops at a time until the emulsion begins to form, then continue adding the rest of the oil in a thin, steady stream. Add the salt and pepper to taste and pulse to blend.

Refrigerate the mayonnaise, covered, until ready to serve; it may be made a day or two in advance.

Makes a generous ¾ cup

The Wild Mushroom Maven

Veronica Williams held up the hawk's wing (*Sarcodon imbricatum*) and spoke animatedly of the milk-chocolate-colored mushroom, akin to the hedgehog but with a sort of scaly effect on the cap that is reminiscent of deeply colored bird feathers. It was the show-and-tell portion of a wild mushroom dinner at the Shoalwater Restaurant on Washington's Long Beach Peninsula, and Williams—a professional forager—was the featured guest of the evening. She brought in a basket of treasures she'd collected earlier that day, testament to the variety of mushrooms available in this seaside habitat and also to her passion for her work.

It's a long way from Hungary's Carpathian Mountains to this windswept seascape, but Veronica Williams made just that trip with her family more than three decades ago. She's so perfectly at home here, you'd think she had been born with one foot in the Pacific Ocean and the other under a Douglas fir poking around for mushrooms.

"Americans are just beginning to scratch the surface of mushroom utilization and understanding," she told us at dinner. As one of those Americans who has become mycologically minded only in recent years, I can attest to that. Williams, on the other hand, has been picking mushrooms since the age of three. She remembers that her family used to yodel a lot while they were picking mushrooms; now she thinks that wasn't just to provide a mushrooming soundtrack but to scare away the bears, a lesson she still takes to heart. Her family picked only the few varieties of mushrooms that they knew well, among them the ever-popular porcini, which tend to grow in fours, "Mom, Dad, and the two kids," as her father put it. To this day, she always looks around for the porcini kin when she finds one specimen.

Williams has added many more mushrooms to her repertoire since settling on the peninsula, among them oyster mushrooms, coral mushrooms, lobster mushrooms, chanterelles, hedgehogs, and matsutakes. She sells her foraged fare to top restaurateurs throughout the region—and as far away as the Tabard Inn in Washington, D.C.—Thierry Rautureau, chef/owner of Rover's restaurant in Seattle among them. "He's one of my best customers," Williams says of Rautureau. They don't exchange phone calls, he places no orders, but she sends some of her harvest to the Rover's kitchen a couple times a week during the peak season. "It's a little like shooting from the hip," Rautureau says. "We never know what we'll get from her, nor when, but I'm always thrilled when I see a new delivery come to the back door. Veronica provides me with some of the best wild mushrooms I've ever seen."

John Newman, chef at the Stephanie Inn in Cannon Beach, Oregon, is another fan of Williams. Not only does he happily incorporate whatever she delivers into his nightly menu, but he used her winter chanterelles in a special dinner of Northwest foods to commemorate the centennial of Portland-born gastronome James Beard's birth. Williams has become quite a legacy in her own right, contributing mightily to the appreciation and availability of wild mushrooms in this region.

Wild Mushroom and Veal Pâté

This recipe is elaborate, but it's a great crowd-pleaser for a special party or elegant dinner. The pâté can be simply sliced and set on crackers or thin slices of baguette with a dab of Dijon mustard on top for great cocktail fare. I also like to serve the pâté with a bit of interesting chutney on top, such as pear or peach. Or the sliced pâté could be a first course, garnished with a little poof of salad—frisée or watercress tossed in a sherry vinaigrette.

You may need to make a special request for ground veal, as it is not always available in grocery store meat sections. Any kind of mushroom may be used here; results are best when you use an assortment, offering a variety of colors and textures. Dried wild mushrooms may be used, though not to completely replace the fresh. Use 1½ pounds of the fresh (cultivated if necessary) with 1 ounce of dried wild mushrooms, reconstituted in hot water, then drained and chopped.

3 tablespoons olive oil
4 shallots, finely chopped
2 pounds wild mushrooms,
    brushed clean, trimmed,
    and coarsely chopped
3 tablespoons brandy

Salt and freshly ground black pepper
1 pound ground lean veal
2 eggs
½ teaspoon minced thyme
Pinch freshly grated or ground nutmeg
1½ cups whipping cream, well chilled

Preheat the oven to 350°F.

Heat the oil in a large skillet over medium heat. Add the shallots and cook until tender and aromatic, 3 to 4 minutes, stirring often. Add the mushrooms and cook, stirring, until they are tender and any liquid they give off has evaporated, 15 to 20 minutes. Drizzle the brandy over and use a long match to carefully light the brandy, shaking the pan very gently until the flames subside. Season to taste with salt and pepper and cook 1 to 2 minutes longer, stirring, to help evaporate excess liquid. Set aside to cool.

Put the veal in a food processor with about half of the cooled sautéed mushrooms and shallots and pulse a few times to blend. Add the eggs, thyme, and nutmeg with a generous pinch of salt and pepper; pulse to mix. Add the chilled cream gradually, pulsing as you go to smoothly incorporate the cream into the veal mousse. Bring a small pan of water to a boil. Add a teaspoonful of the veal mousse to the water and poach until it is firm and cooked through, about 1 minute, then let it cool slightly. Taste this sample for seasoning, adding more salt or pepper to the remaining mousse if needed.

Transfer the mousse to a large bowl and stir in the remaining mushrooms and shallots.

Spoon the mixture into a pâté mold or a 9-by-5-inch loaf pan, preferably nonmetallic, pressing down well as you fill the mold to avoid gaps or air pockets. Cover securely with the lid or with foil. Set the mold in a larger baking dish and half-fill the baking dish with boiling water. Transfer the pans to the oven and bake until a thermometer inserted in the center reads 165°F (or a metal skewer inserted for a few seconds is very hot to the touch), about 1½ hours.

Take the pâté mold from the water bath and let cool to room temperature. Drain off any accumulated liquid from the pâté, then cover securely with plastic and refrigerate the pâté until ready to serve; the flavor will be more developed if it is made a day before you plan to serve it.

Turn the pâté out onto a serving platter and serve, allowing your guests to cut their own slices, or invert the pâté onto a cutting board for slicing to serve.

Makes 10 to 12 servings

Roasted Morels Stuffed with Leeks and Walnuts

A great option for dinner-party fare, the mushrooms may be roasted and filled in advance, then finished in the oven just before serving. The stuffed mushrooms make tasty finger food to offer on a buffet table, or they could also be dressed up to serve sit-down style, arranging 3 morels on a small salad of mesclun greens tossed with a vinaigrette dressing, preferably using walnut oil. Other wild mushrooms don't lend themselves to stuffing the way that morels do. You could instead sauté 8 ounces of chopped wild mushrooms and stir them into the leek and walnut mixture, spreading this on sliced baguette to broil and serve as an elegant crostini.

¼ cup walnut pieces
12 large morel mushrooms
  (6 to 8 ounces)
3 tablespoons olive oil
Salt and freshly ground
  black pepper

2 leeks, split, cleaned, and
  finely chopped
2 ounces cream cheese,
  at room temperature
2 tablespoons freshly grated
  Parmesan cheese

Preheat the oven to 350°F. Scatter the walnuts in a baking pan and toast in the oven until lightly browned and aromatic, about 5 to 7 minutes, gently shaking the pan once or twice to help the nuts toast evenly. Transfer the nuts to a small dish and let cool. Increase the oven temperature to 425°F.

Put the mushrooms in a medium bowl, drizzle 1 tablespoon of the olive oil over, and season with a good pinch of salt and pepper. Toss gently to coat, arrange the morels in the baking pan, and roast in the oven until tender and aromatic, 8 to 10 minutes. Set the mushrooms aside to cool. Leave the oven set at 425°F.

While the mushrooms are cooling, heat the remaining 2 tablespoons olive oil in a medium skillet over medium heat. Add the leeks and cook until tender and aromatic, 3 to 5 minutes. Take the skillet from the heat and let cool. Finely chop the toasted walnuts and add them to the leeks. Trim the stems from the morels, finely chop the stems and add them to the skillet with the cream cheese and Parmesan cheese. Stir the mixture well until it is evenly blended, seasoning to taste with salt and pepper.

Using a small knife, cut open one side of each morel. Use a small spoon to fill each morel and arrange them slit-side up on the baking pan. Roast just until heated through, 3 to 5 minutes. Arrange the morels on a serving platter and serve right away.

Makes 4 to 6 servings

Focaccia with Wild Mushrooms and Rosemary

This somewhat unusual variation on the well-loved flatbread from Italy adds some sautéed wild mushrooms to the rosemary-enhanced dough. The technique for cooking the mushrooms is dry-sautéing, cooking them in a skillet without any oil. The mushrooms will give off their liquid to moisten the pan, then the liquid will evaporate and leave the mushrooms cooked through but not oily, which will help them blend into the focaccia dough more easily. This great aperitif snack is especially delicious with a really good glass of wine: the herbal and earthy flavors of the bread would be ideal with a full-bodied wine, or bubbly is always perfect. Tender mushrooms such as chanterelles, oysters, or hedgehogs are ideal in this recipe.

8 ounces wild mushrooms, brushed clean, trimmed, and finely chopped

1 teaspoon minced garlic

2 cups all-purpose flour

1 teaspoon salt

½ teaspoon freshly ground black pepper

¾ cup warm water (about 105°F)

2 teaspoons (1 envelope) active dry yeast

3 tablespoons olive oil

2 teaspoons minced fresh rosemary

2 to 3 tablespoons grated Parmesan cheese (optional)

Heat a medium skillet, preferably nonstick, over medium heat, then add the mushrooms and cook, stirring occasionally, until they begin to give off their liquid, 3 to 5 minutes. Add the minced garlic and continue sautéing until the liquid has evaporated and the mushrooms are quite dry. Take the pan from the heat, season the mushrooms with salt and pepper, and set aside to cool.

Put the flour in a medium bowl, making a well in the center. Along the outer edge of the well, make a small indentation in the flour (I use the handle of a measuring spoon to draw the flour away from the side of the bowl) and put the salt and pepper into that pocket (they shouldn't come in contact with the yeast while it's proofing). Pour the warm water into the well and sprinkle the yeast over. Set aside until the yeast is frothy, about 5 minutes.

Stir the dough for a few seconds, gently drawing in the flour from the edges, then drizzle the olive oil over and sprinkle in the rosemary. Continue to stir the dough until it just begins to come together, then add the mushrooms and continue mixing until the dough is cohesive and forms a ball. Transfer it to a lightly floured work surface and knead the dough until it becomes smooth and satiny, about 10 minutes. Put the dough in a lightly oiled bowl (it could be the same bowl you mixed the dough in) and turn it to evenly but lightly coat the dough with oil. Cover the bowl with a clean kitchen towel and set aside in a warm place until the dough has risen by half, about 1 hour.

Lightly oil a heavy baking sheet. Turn the risen dough out onto a lightly floured work surface and gently knead it to deflate. Using your palms, press the dough out into a rectangle the size of your baking sheet. Fold the dough into quarters and transfer it to the baking sheet, unfolding it to fit. Cover the pan with the towel and set aside to rise again by about half, 45 to 60 minutes.

Preheat the oven to 375°F.

Sprinkle the Parmesan cheese over the dough, if using, and bake the focaccia until nicely browned on the bottom and lightly browned on top, 18 to 20 minutes. Let cool on a wire rack, then cut the focaccia in half lengthwise and across into individual pieces.

Makes 8 servings

Marinated Wild Mushrooms with Fennel and Pearl Onions

Choose firmer mushrooms that will retain toothsome texture after marinating—porcini, lobster, cauliflower, and such; chanterelles and other tender mushrooms become quite soft in this preparation. The marinated mushrooms and vegetables make a tasty snack for cocktail hour, or can be served as an appetizer in individual dishes, with crusty bread alongside. This dish is also a delicious picnic element, with cold roasted chicken, hearty cheeses, and a bright chilled bottle of rosé wine. The flavor of this dish will be best if made at least a few hours in advance so the seasonings have a chance to meld with the mushrooms.

2 tablespoons coriander seeds
2 bay leaves
1 tablespoon fennel seeds
1 tablespoon black peppercorns
3 sprigs thyme
2 sprigs flat-leaf (Italian) parsley
2 cloves garlic, crushed
1 to 1½ pounds mixed wild mushrooms, brushed clean and trimmed

2 tablespoons olive oil
15 pearl onions, peeled whole
1 medium fennel bulb, trimmed, cored, and thinly sliced
3 medium tomatoes, peeled, seeded, and finely chopped (see box)
1 cup chicken or vegetable stock
½ cup white wine vinegar
Salt and freshly ground black pepper

Cut a double-thickness piece of cheesecloth about 6 inches square and set it on the work surface. In the center of the cheesecloth, put the coriander seeds, bay leaves, fennel

---

Peeling and Seeding Tomatoes: Bring a medium saucepan half-filled with water to a boil. On the bottom of each tomato, make a small X with the tip of a knife. When the water's at a full boil, add the tomato(es) and watch for the skin to begin to split. When it does (it can be a matter of just a few seconds or up to 30 seconds, depending on the type and ripeness of the tomato), scoop the tomato(es) out with a slotted spoon and let cool on a plate. When cool enough to handle, the skin will peel away very easily. To seed the tomato, cut it in half crosswise and scoop out the seeds with your fingers or with a small spoon.

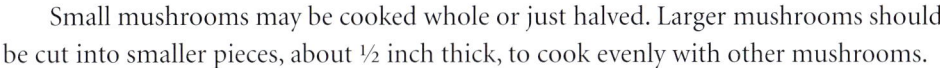

seeds, peppercorns, thyme, parsley, and garlic. Draw up the cloth around the spices and tie the packet securely with kitchen string.

Small mushrooms may be cooked whole or just halved. Larger mushrooms should be cut into smaller pieces, about ½ inch thick, to cook evenly with other mushrooms.

In a medium sauté pan or deep skillet, heat the olive oil over medium heat. Add the onions and cook until they are lightly browned and just beginning to soften, about 5 minutes, stirring occasionally. Add the mushrooms, fennel, and tomatoes and stir to mix, then add the spice bag with the stock, vinegar, and a good pinch each of salt and pepper. Bring the mixture just to a boil over medium-high heat, then reduce the heat to medium-low and simmer gently until the vegetables are tender and the cooking liquids have reduced by at least half, about 30 minutes.

Take the pan from the heat and let cool, then transfer the mixture (spice bag included) to a glass or ceramic bowl and refrigerate, covered, for at least 4 hours or overnight. Before serving, allow the marinated mushroom mixture to come to room temperature, discard the spice bag, and check for seasoning, adding more salt or pepper to taste.

Makes 6 to 8 servings

Pan-Seared Razor Clams and Chanterelles with Brown Butter

The season for razor clams is limited, with occasional openings through the winter and early spring, making fresh clams available sporadically. Some stores carry frozen razor clams, though the pasta with chanterelles and hazelnuts is delicious as is, or serve it instead with pan-seared scallops or steamed and shelled Manila clams.

1 cup orzo pasta or other small
    pasta shape

6 tablespoons unsalted butter

8 ounces chanterelles, brushed clean,
    trimmed, and halved or quartered

Salt and freshly ground
    black pepper

8 ounces cleaned razor clams, drained,
    patted dry, and quartered

½ cup all-purpose flour

¼ cup finely chopped toasted
    hazelnuts

2 tablespoons freshly squeezed
    lemon juice

Bring a medium saucepan of salted water to a boil, add the pasta, and cook until al dente, 8 to 10 minutes. Drain well and set aside.

Melt 4 tablespoons of the butter in a large skillet, preferably nonstick, over medium heat and continue to cook until the butter turns a medium brown and smells slightly nutty (known as "brown butter"), 3 to 5 minutes. Gently add the mushrooms to the skillet and cook, stirring often, until they are tender, 3 to 5 minutes. Season the mushrooms to taste with salt and pepper, then transfer them to a bowl and set aside.

Razor Clams: Unlike other key clam species in the Northwest, razor clams are not farm-raised but are available only in the wild on the surf-swept beaches of the Pacific Coast. I've seen pros dig bare-handed for the prized bivalves, though most sport clammers use the "clam gun" (a specially designed digging tube) to capture the astonishingly quick razor clam before it digs too deep into the sand. A popular recreational shellfish, razor clams are also distributed commercially, which means that the rest of us can buy them, either in the shell or shucked and cleaned, at local seafood markets. Availability can be unpredictable, however, so call around before shopping.

Add the remaining 2 tablespoons of butter to the skillet and cook it also until medium brown and nutty smelling. While the butter is melting, season the razor clams with salt and pepper and quickly toss them in the flour to evenly coat, patting to remove excess flour. When the brown butter is ready, increase the heat to medium-high and add the razor clams. Cook just until browned on each side but still tender, about 30 seconds per side. Return the mushrooms and any juices to the skillet with the hazelnuts, lemon juice, and cooked orzo. Toss quickly just to combine and gently warm the pasta, check for seasoning, then transfer to individual plates and serve right away.

Makes 4 servings

Northwest Meurette

Like many of my favorite things to cook at home, this recipe is inspired by my time in France. While in college, I spent a semester studying at the University of Dijon in the heart of the celebrated Burgundy wine-making region. Based on the classic rustic Burgundian dish, *oeufs en meurette,* this recipe makes an unexpected pairing of eggs with red wine, which serves both as the poaching liquid and the base for the sauce that is accented with mushrooms, bacon, and onions. One egg per person suffices for an appetizer serving, but you could serve two eggs per person for a hearty main course as well.

Really any mushroom will be at home in this recipe; firmer mushrooms such as lobsters will maintain a meatier texture, while chanterelles or hedgehogs will be softer. "Red wine" in Burgundy means pinot noir. The lighter, fruitier pinot noir wines common in the Northwest wouldn't be as well-suited as the more robust French style. Merlot would be a better regional option.

4 thick strips bacon, cut into
  ¼-inch pieces
6 ounces red pearl onions,
  peeled whole
¾ pound wild mushrooms,
  brushed clean, trimmed,
  and coarsely chopped

1 bottle (750 ml) robust red wine
¼ cup red wine vinegar
6 eggs
2 tablespoons unsalted butter,
  at room temperature
2 tablespoons all-purpose flour
12 baguette slices, toasted

Cook the bacon in a medium saucepan over medium heat until beginning to brown and some of the fat is rendered, 1 to 2 minutes. Add the onions and continue cooking, stirring often, until the onions are nearly tender, about 5 minutes longer. Remove all but 2 tablespoons of the fat from the pan. Add the mushrooms and sauté, stirring occasionally, until tender and any liquid they give off has evaporated, about 5 minutes longer. Set the saucepan aside while poaching the eggs.

Combine the red wine and vinegar in a large skillet over medium-high heat. When the liquid just starts to boil, reduce the heat to medium and carefully crack the eggs into the wine. (To avoid scalding your knuckles, you could first crack each egg into a small bowl, then gently tip the egg from the bowl into the wine.) Simmer gently until the egg whites are set and the yolks are still soft, 3 to 4 minutes, gently sloshing some of the wine over the top of the eggs once or twice during cooking to help set the surface of the yolks. Scoop out the eggs with a slotted spoon and drain them on a plate lined with paper towels.

Strain the poaching liquid into the mushroom mixture in the saucepan, return it to medium-high heat, and bring to a boil. Combine the butter and flour in a small bowl and stir well to make a smooth paste. Add the butter paste to the red wine sauce, stirring constantly as it cooks until thickened, 3 to 5 minutes. Season the sauce to taste with salt and pepper.

Arrange 2 baguette slices side by side on each plate and set a poached egg on top of the toast. Spoon the red wine sauce over the eggs and serve right away.

Makes 6 servings

Soups, Salads, and Side Dishes

Potato Leek Soup with Oven-Roasted Wild Mushrooms

A rich, hot soup is just the thing to start the thaw after a chilly day out on the slopes, hiking, or to revive you after any of the great Northwest activities (even if it's just reading a good book). Any variety of wild mushrooms would be tasty in this dish.

4 tablespoons olive oil

4 large leeks, white and pale
 green parts only, split, cleaned,
 and chopped

3 large russet potatoes
 (about 3 pounds), peeled
 and cut into chunks

Salt and freshly ground
 black pepper

6 cups chicken stock

2 teaspoons minced sage,
 plus 1 big sprig

8 ounces wild mushrooms,
 brushed clean, trimmed,
 and coarsely chopped

1 tablespoon minced chives or
 flat-leaf (Italian) parsley

½ cup whipping cream or
 half-and-half

2 tablespoons dry vermouth

Preheat the oven to 450°F.

In a soup pot or large saucepan, heat 2 tablespoons of the oil over medium heat. Add the leeks and cook, stirring, until aromatic and they begin to soften, 2 to 3 minutes. Stir in the potato chunks with a generous pinch of salt and pepper and stir to mix with the leeks. Add the chicken stock with the sage sprig and bring just to a boil, then lower the heat and simmer until the potatoes are very tender, 20 to 30 minutes.

While the soup is simmering, put the mushrooms in a medium bowl and drizzle the remaining 2 tablespoons of olive oil over, tossing to evenly coat. Add the chives, minced sage, and a good pinch of salt and pepper and toss to mix. Transfer the mixture to an ovenproof skillet and roast in the oven until the mushrooms are tender and lightly crisped around the edges, 15 to 20 minutes.

When the potatoes are tender, remove the sage sprig from the pot and purée the soup using an immersion blender or working in batches in a food processor. Return the soup to medium heat and taste for seasoning, adding more salt or pepper to taste.

Ladle the hot soup into individual bowls and spoon the roasted wild mushrooms into the center of the soup. Add the cream to the skillet that the mushrooms were cooked in and bring to a boil over medium-high heat, stirring to scrape up flavorful bits stuck to the skillet and reduce the liquid to thicken slightly, 1 to 2 minutes. Add the vermouth and boil for 1 minute longer, then season to taste with salt and pepper. Drizzle the cream mixture over the surface of the soups and serve right away.

Makes 4 to 6 servings

Sukiyaki with Matsutake

Sukiyaki loosely translates as "broiled on the blade of a plow," though modern interpretations of this classic Japanese dish are no longer broiled despite its "yaki" name (think teriyaki). It is traditionally a *nabemono* dish ("cooked at the table") and classified as a *nimono* dish as well, meaning that the ingredients are cooked in seasoned liquid. My variation on the recipe is a break with tradition, prepared fully in the kitchen rather than at the table—which I find easier. *Shirataki* noodles are precooked and sold refrigerated, packed in liquid, available at Asian markets and gourmet grocery stores. If you can't find *shirataki* noodles, boil some udon noodles until tender, then drain well. Sukiyaki is traditionally a lightly sweetened dish, though you may omit the sugar if you prefer. Oyster, porcini, or lobster mushrooms would be good alternatives to the matsutakes.

2 cups beef stock

½ cup sake

¼ cup soy sauce

1 bunch green onions, trimmed

1 piece beef suet, about 2 inches long,
    or 2 tablespoons unsalted butter

½ small yellow onion,
    cut into ½-inch wedges

8 ounces green cabbage,
    cored and shredded

8 ounces matsutake mushrooms,
    brushed clean, trimmed, and sliced

8 ounces *shirataki* (taro noodles),
    cut into 5-inch pieces

1 packet (about 11 ounces)
    firm tofu, cubed

1½ pounds very thinly sliced marbled
    beef, preferably wagyu-style
    (see box page 52)

2 to 3 tablespoons sugar (optional)

Combine the stock, sake, and soy sauce in a large saucepan and warm over medium heat while cooking the vegetables. Thinly slice enough of the green onion tops to make ¼ cup; set aside for garnish. Cut the remaining green onions in half crosswise.

Heat a wok or a large heavy skillet, such as cast iron, over medium-high heat. When hot, rub the beef suet over the surface of the pan to evenly coat it with fat, then remove, or simply add the butter and let it melt. Add the green onion pieces, yellow onion, cabbage, and matsutakes and stir-fry until they begin to soften, 3 to 5 minutes. Transfer the vegetables to the broth mixture, add the noodles and tofu cubes, and keep warm over low heat.

Add 3 or 4 of the beef slices to the wok and cook quickly, just until nicely browned, 30 to 60 seconds on each side, drizzling about 2 tablespoons of the warm broth and 1 teaspoon of the sugar over when you turn the meat. Press these pieces to one side of the wok and continue with the remaining meat, which will gently simmer in the collecting liquids. When all of the meat has been cooked, take the wok from the heat.

To serve, ladle the hot broth, mushrooms, tofu, and vegetables into individual bowls, top with the beef slices and drizzle some of the cooking liquids over. Sprinkle with a final garnish of green onion and serve right away.

Makes 4 servings

Wagyu beef is a more generic term for the celebrated Kobe beef (a place-specific name for beef produced in that part of Japan, much like Champagne in France). Based on the specific wagyu breed of cattle, what they're fed, and how they're raised, the meat produced has an elaborate marbling of fat throughout the lean flesh, which makes for enormously flavorful and tender results when cooked. Some American ranches are producing wagyu beef, available in many Asian markets or other specialty stores along the West Coast. In fact, you may find it (as I do) already cut into very thin slices perfect for this recipe. If you can't find wagyu beef, choose a well-marbled piece of beef and cut it into very thin slices (a brief stay in the freezer to firm up the meat will make slicing easier).

Wild Rice and Wild Mushroom Soup

Dried wild mushrooms are a particularly good choice for this soup, as their heady concentrated flavor is a welcome complement to the nutty wild rice. In fact, fresh mushrooms can be omitted altogether, making this a great off-season choice.

The variety of mushroom you use is up to you; sometimes a mix of different dried mushrooms is available in a single packet, which is a great option. A bonus is the flavorful liquid produced by the mushrooms when they are reconstituted in hot water, which makes a tasty contribution to the soup as well.

2½ cups cold water
2 bay leaves
Salt and freshly ground black pepper
1 cup wild rice
1½ ounces dried wild mushrooms
   (1 ounce if using fresh mushrooms
   as well)
1½ cups hot water
3 tablespoons unsalted butter

2 large leeks, white and pale green
   parts only, split, cleaned, and finely
   chopped, or 2 cups finely
   chopped onion
8 ounces wild mushrooms, brushed
   clean, trimmed, and chopped
   (optional)
2 teaspoons minced thyme or
   ½ teaspoon dried thyme
1 quart chicken or vegetable stock
¾ cup whipping cream or
   half-and-half

Combine the cold water with the bay leaves and ½ teaspoon salt in a medium saucepan and bring to a boil over high heat. Stir in the wild rice, reduce the heat to medium-low, and simmer gently, uncovered, until the rice is tender and most of the liquid has been absorbed, about 1 hour. Drain any remaining water from the rice, discard the bay leaves, and set aside.

Put the dried mushrooms in a small bowl and pour the hot water over. Set aside until softened and cool, about 30 minutes. Drain the mushrooms, reserving the liquid, and finely chop the mushrooms, setting both aside.

Melt the butter in a large saucepan over medium heat. Add the leeks, fresh mushrooms (if using), and thyme. Cook, stirring often, until the leeks and mushrooms are tender, 3 to 5 minutes. Add the stock with the wild rice, dried mushrooms, and their soaking liquid (leaving any gritty bits behind in the bottom of the bowl). Simmer, uncovered, for 30 minutes, allowing the flavors to meld. Using an immersion blender, whir the soup with 4 or 5 pulses to purée some of the soup, leaving most of the rice and other ingredients as is for texture. (Alternatively, ladle about one-third of the soup into a food processor or blender to purée, then return it to the soup pot.) Stir in the cream and season the soup to taste with salt and pepper. Ladle the soup into individual bowls and serve right away.

Makes 4 to 6 servings

Warm Spinach Salad with Wild Mushrooms, Bacon, and Hazelnuts

A few delightfully earthy-rich flavors come together in this salad: wild mushrooms, toasted hazelnuts, smoky bacon. This dish is a tasty twist on the classic warm spinach salad.

1 pound spinach, rinsed, dried, and tough stems removed
4 thick strips bacon, cut into ½-inch pieces
¼ cup thinly sliced shallots

8 ounces wild mushrooms, brushed clean, trimmed, and halved (or quartered if large)
¼ cup red wine vinegar
1 tablespoon hazelnut oil
Salt and freshly ground black pepper
⅓ cup chopped toasted hazelnuts

Put the spinach in a salad bowl or other large bowl, tearing any large spinach leaves into 2 or 3 pieces.

Heat a large skillet over medium heat, add the bacon pieces and cook, stirring occasionally, until browned and crisp, 5 to 7 minutes. Scoop out the bacon pieces with a slotted spoon and drain on paper towels, leaving the bacon fat in the skillet. Add the shallots and cook, stirring, until tender and aromatic, 2 to 3 minutes. Add the mushrooms and cook, stirring often, until tender and any liquid they give off has evaporated by about half, 3 to 5 minutes. Take the skillet from the heat and stir in the vinegar and hazelnut oil with salt and pepper to taste.

Add the mushroom mixture, bacon, and hazelnuts to the spinach and quickly toss to evenly mix. Arrange the salad on individual plates and serve right away.

Makes 4 servings

When "Wild" Mushrooms Aren't

A big pet peeve of mine is misuse of the term "wild mushroom." It's disappointing to order a wild mushroom risotto only to find the creamy-delicious rice speckled not with chanterelles, hedgehogs, or morels, but with shiitakes, crimini, or portobello. While those latter three varieties have exotic-sounding names and certainly can be delicious, they are not actually wild mushrooms. The crimini and portobello are variations on the ubiquitous white button mushroom *(Agaricus bisporus)* so common in grocery stores—the portobello a much more mature version, the crimini a button with a brown-hued, rather than white, cap. The shiitake mushroom may still be harvested wild in Japan, but it is not a species that is known to have been collected wild in North America; even in Japan it has been cultivated for centuries.

There is plenty of culinary room for "gourmet" or "exotic" mushrooms—cultivated types that stand out from the standard button by offering a variety of flavor and texture options. They're raised commercially and sold in stores throughout the year, and are a good off-season alternative to wild mushrooms. You can even buy kits to grow many of these mushrooms at home, a surprisingly easy prospect. However, just a handful of familiar wild mushrooms are sold in these kits, including oyster, lion's mane, and hen of the woods, while others are mushroom types more specifically developed for cultivation.

There is no governing agency that has set any standards for use of the term "wild mushroom" so chefs can use the term freely. But I'll still hope that more menus will begin to specify mushrooms by name, or at least call them by some other more appropriate moniker when "wild" they're not.

Sesame Steak Salad with Soy-Glazed Oyster Mushrooms

Flank steak has long been one of my favorite cuts of beef, which my mother typically cooked up teriyaki-style when I was growing up. Using that memory as a starting point for this recipe, slices of the grilled steak embellish a crisp romaine salad that's tossed with an Asian-style vinaigrette. Tender oyster mushrooms sautéed with a bronze glaze adorn the salad with style. Other wild mushrooms could be used as well, particularly tender varieties such as chanterelle or hedgehog.

3 tablespoons soy sauce
3 tablespoons vegetable oil
2 tablespoons mirin (sweet rice wine)
¾ pound oyster mushrooms,
    brushed clean and trimmed
1 flank steak (about 1¼ pounds)

1 tablespoon sesame oil
Salt and freshly ground black pepper
1 head romaine lettuce, rinsed, dried,
    and torn into pieces
1 tablespoon toasted sesame seeds

Vinaigrette

3 tablespoons rice wine vinegar or
    white wine vinegar
1 green onion, minced
1 clove garlic, minced

⅓ cup vegetable oil
2 teaspoons soy sauce
1 teaspoon sesame oil

For the vinaigrette, combine the vinegar, green onion, and garlic in a small bowl. Whisk in the vegetable oil, followed by the soy sauce and sesame oil. Set aside.

Combine the soy sauce, 2 tablespoons of the vegetable oil, and the mirin in a medium bowl and stir to mix. If any of the mushrooms is large, cut them in half. Add the mushrooms to the soy sauce marinade and toss to evenly coat them. Let sit for 15 minutes, tossing the mushrooms 3 or 4 times.

Preheat an outdoor grill or the broiler.

Lightly score the flank steak on both sides in a diamond pattern and rub the steak with the sesame oil, then season with salt and pepper. Grill or broil the steak 3 to 4 minutes per side for medium-rare, about 5 minutes per side for medium, or longer to suit your taste. Transfer the steak to a cutting board and let sit for about 10 minutes, covered loosely with foil to keep warm.

While the steak is resting, heat the remaining tablespoon of vegetable oil in a wok or large skillet over medium-high heat. When the oil is hot, add the mushrooms with the marinade and stir-fry until tender, any liquid they give off has evaporated, and the glaze is lightly browned, 3 to 5 minutes.

To serve, put the romaine in a large bowl. Rewhisk the vinaigrette to mix and drizzle it over the lettuce with the sesame seeds. Toss well, then arrange the greens on 4 plates. Cut the flank steak into ¼-inch slices at a slight angle and lay the slices over the greens. Top the steak with the glazed mushrooms and serve right away.

Makes 4 servings

Harvest Barley Salad

The light, nutty flavor of barley blends beautifully with the earthiness of mushrooms, accented by hazelnuts and tart-sweet dried cranberries or cherries. This dish would be ideal alongside roasted pork or chicken, or at lunchtime with cheese and bread. The salad will be at its best if made at least a few hours in advance, allowing the flavors to meld and develop before serving. If you're in a big hurry, you may skip soaking the barley and simply cook it in boiling water for about 20 minutes, but the texture is better if soaked before cooking.

1 pound wild mushrooms, brushed
   clean, trimmed, and coarsely
   chopped, or 2 ounces dried
   wild mushrooms
1 cup barley
2 tablespoons olive oil
1 medium onion, finely chopped
2 tablespoons minced flat-leaf
   (Italian) parsley

1 teaspoon chopped thyme
¾ cup hazelnuts, toasted and
   coarsely chopped
½ cup chopped dried cranberries
   or cherries
Salt and freshly ground
   black pepper

Soak the barley in a large bowl of cold water (enough to generously cover the grain) for 4 to 5 hours, or overnight in the refrigerator, stirring occasionally.

If using dried mushrooms, put them in a small heatproof bowl and pour about 1½ cups boiling water over. Set aside until tender and cool, about 30 minutes. Drain the mushrooms, reserving the liquid. Finely chop the mushrooms and set aside.

When ready to cook the barley, bring a large pan of salted water to a boil. Drain the barley and add it to the boiling water. Cook over medium-high heat until the barley is just tender but still has a slight bite, 15 to 20 minutes.

While the barley is cooking, heat the olive oil in a large skillet over medium heat. Add the onion and cook, stirring, until tender and aromatic, 3 to 5 minutes. Add the fresh mushrooms and continue cooking, stirring often, until the mushrooms are tender and any liquid they give off has evaporated, 5 to 7 minutes. (If using reconstituted dried mushrooms, simply cook them until heated through, 1 to 2 minutes.)

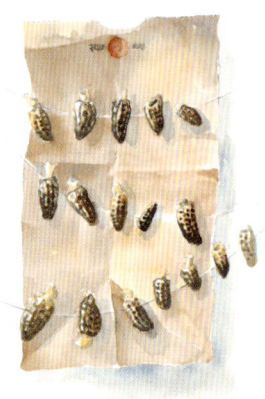

Take the skillet from the heat and stir in the parsley and thyme. When the barley is cooked, drain it well and add it to the skillet with the hazelnuts and dried cranberries or cherries, stirring to evenly mix. (If using dried mushrooms, stir in about ½ cup of the mushroom soaking liquid as well.) Season the salad to taste with salt and pepper. Let cool, then cover and refrigerate until ready to serve.

Makes 6 to 8 servings

Grilled Wild Mushrooms on Rosemary Skewers

The woody stems of rosemary make great skewers for grilling. Not only are they sturdy enough to hold most foods, but the stems impart flavor as the food cooks. Wild mushrooms particularly benefit from the woodsy, aromatic flavor of rosemary. This recipe is ideal alongside grilled steaks or burgers, but could also become a vegetarian main course served over rice, perhaps with grilled corn. If you're unable to find long, sturdy rosemary sprigs, you may use bamboo skewers instead. A wide range of mushrooms may be used for this recipe, keeping in mind that firmer, longer cooking varieties should be cut into smaller pieces to better coincide with the cooking time of more delicate varieties.

6 long, sturdy sprigs rosemary
  (8 to 10 inches long)
4 tablespoons olive oil
2 tablespoons dry white wine
  or vermouth

2 cloves garlic, minced
Salt and freshly ground
  black pepper
1 pound mixed wild mushrooms,
  brushed clean and trimmed

Strip most of the rosemary leaves from the sprigs (saving some for the marinade), leaving the top inch or so of leaves for a visual flourish. Soak the sprigs in cold water while preparing the mushrooms.

Finely mince enough of the rosemary leaves to make 1 tablespoon and put it in a large bowl with the olive oil, wine, garlic, and a good pinch each of salt and pepper. Stir to blend. (The remaining rosemary can be saved for another use or discarded.)

Cut the mushrooms into pieces so that they will cook evenly: tender chanterelles or oyster mushrooms can be larger than denser porcini or lobster mushrooms, for instance. Add the mushrooms to the bowl and toss gently to evenly coat them in the oil. Set aside for about 15 minutes to marinate, then thread the mushrooms onto the rosemary skewers, distributing different types of mushrooms evenly among the skewers.

Preheat an outdoor grill.

When the grill is hot, lightly brush the grill grate with oil. Lay the skewers on the grill and cook until the mushrooms are tender and the edges are lightly crispy-brown, about 2 minutes per side. Serve right away.

Makes 6 servings

Braised Wild Mushrooms and Winter Greens with Golden Beets

The leafy tops from a bunch of beets will make up some of the braising greens needed for this dish. If you're unable to find beets with their greens attached, increase the quantity of other greens to 1½ pounds. Some markets sell a mix of "braising greens" with a combination of different types. When cleaning greens that tend to be gritty (as these do), I fill a sink with cold water and soak the leaves for a few minutes, then swish them around by the handful in the water to help dislodge any remaining grit and lift them from the water to a salad spinner basket or layers of paper towel. This recipe would make a good vegetarian main course or a side dish for pork chops or fried chicken. You may use red beets in place of golden.

1 bunch golden beets, greens attached
   (about 1½ pounds)
1 pound braising greens (kale, mustard
   greens, escarole, and/or Swiss chard)
4 tablespoons unsalted butter
8 ounces chanterelles, brushed clean
   and sliced

1 cup thinly sliced leeks
   or onion
¼ cup vegetable stock or
   dry white wine
Salt and freshly ground
   black pepper
2 to 3 tablespoons red wine vinegar

Preheat the oven to 350°F.

Cut the leafy greens from the beets and set aside. Trim the tops and root ends from the beets and rinse them, then pat dry with paper towels. Set the beets in the center of a large piece of doubled-up foil and enclose them tightly in the foil. Roast the beets until they are tender (they'll "give" a bit when you squeeze them, like a baked potato), about 1 hour. Set the packet aside to cool completely, then unwrap the beets and peel away and discard the skin. Cut each roasted beet in half, then across into half-moon slices about ¼ inch thick. Set aside in a bowl.

Thoroughly rinse the beet tops and other braising greens, shaking off excess water. Cut the greens (including the stems) crosswise into roughly 2-inch strips.

Melt the butter in a sauté pan or deep skillet over medium heat and continue to cook until the butter turns a medium brown and smells slightly nutty (known as "brown butter"), about 5 minutes. Add the mushrooms and leeks and sauté until tender and the mushrooms begin to give off some of their liquid, 3 to 5 minutes. Add the greens a handful or two at a time, stirring until they begin to wilt before adding the next bunch. When all the greens have been added, reduce the heat to medium-low and pour in the stock. Season generously with salt and pepper, then partly cover the pan and braise the greens until they are tender, about 10 minutes, stirring once or twice. Add the beets to the pan with vinegar to taste, tossing to evenly mix and to allow the beets to heat through. Spoon the braised mushrooms, greens, and beets onto individual plates and serve.

Makes 4 servings

Green Bean and Chanterelle Casserole

Ah, that timeless classic that appears on many holiday tables! This version is dressed up a bit with a freshly made white sauce and plump, delicious chanterelle mushrooms in place of the traditional cream of mushroom soup.

1½ pounds green beans, trimmed
2 tablespoons unsalted butter
2 leeks, white and pale green parts
   only, split, cleaned, and sliced

1 pound chanterelles, brushed clean,
   trimmed, and coarsely chopped
½ cup dry white wine
½ cup dried bread crumbs

White Sauce

3 tablespoons unsalted butter
3 tablespoons all-purpose flour
1½ cups milk

Pinch nutmeg
Salt and freshly ground
   black pepper

For the white sauce, melt the butter in a small saucepan over medium heat. Whisk in the flour and cook, whisking constantly, until the mixture foams up and begins to smell slightly nutty, 2 to 3 minutes (the flour should not brown). Slowly whisk in the milk and cook until the sauce thickens, whisking often to avoid any lumps or sticking, 6 to 8 minutes. Take the pan from the heat and whisk in the nutmeg with salt and pepper to taste. Set aside.

Preheat the oven to 350°F. Generously butter a 12-inch oval baking dish or other 2-quart baking dish. Bring a large pan of salted water to a boil, add the green beans, and cook until they are bright green and nearly tender, 3 to 5 minutes. Drain well.

Melt the butter in a sauté pan or large skillet over medium heat. Add the leeks and cook, stirring, until tender and aromatic, 2 to 3 minutes. Set aside about ½ cup of the chanterelles and add the rest to the skillet. Cook, stirring often, until the mushrooms are tender and any liquid they give off has evaporated, 5 to 7 minutes. Take the skillet from the heat and stir in the white sauce, white wine, and salt and pepper to taste. Add the beans and stir to evenly coat them in the sauce, then transfer the mixture to the prepared baking dish.

Pulse the bread crumbs and reserved chanterelles in a food processor to a fine crumbly texture. Scatter the mixture over the green beans and bake until bubbly-hot and the topping is nicely browned, 30 to 40 minutes. Spoon onto individual plates to serve.

Makes 6 to 8 servings

Potato and Wild Mushroom Gratin

The rich-and-creamy quality of a good potato gratin is deliciously embellished with wild mushrooms sandwiched between layers of thinly sliced potato. If you have a mandolin slicer, it's just the tool to make quick and easy work of slicing the potatoes uniformly. Any type of wild mushroom will be good for this recipe, a few different ones used together even better.

3 tablespoons unsalted butter
½ cup minced shallot or onion
1 teaspoon minced garlic
1 pound wild mushrooms, brushed
   clean, trimmed, and thinly sliced
1 teaspoon minced thyme

Salt and freshly ground
   black pepper
2 pounds russet potatoes
¾ cup grated Parmesan cheese
1 cup whipping cream
1 cup half-and-half

Preheat the oven to 375°F. Generously butter a 12-inch oval gratin dish or other shallow 2-quart baking dish.

Melt the butter in a large skillet over medium heat, add ¼ cup of the shallot and the garlic and sauté until tender and aromatic, 2 to 3 minutes. Add the mushrooms and sauté until they are tender and any liquid they release has evaporated, 10 to 12 minutes. Take the skillet from the heat and stir in the thyme with salt and pepper to taste. Set aside to cool.

Peel the potatoes and cut them into ⅛-inch slices. Sprinkle about half of the remaining shallot over the bottom of the gratin dish and top with about one third of the potato slices, slightly overlapping in an even layer. Season the potatoes with salt and pepper. Top with half of the mushroom mixture, spreading it out evenly, and sprinkle with one third of the Parmesan cheese. Top with another third of the potato slices, the remaining mushrooms, and another third of the Parmesan cheese. Finish with the remaining potatoes, arranging the slices in an attractive pattern.

Stir together the cream and half-and-half in a small bowl, then pour the cream mixture evenly over the potatoes. Sprinkle the remaining shallot and cheese over, seasoning once again with salt and pepper. Set the baking dish on a rimmed baking sheet to catch any drips and bake until the edges of the gratin are bubbling and the potatoes are quite tender (pierce through the layers with a small knife to check), about 1 hour 15 minutes. If the top is well browned before the potatoes are tender, top the gratin loosely with a piece of buttered foil. Let sit for a few minutes before scooping out to serve.

Makes 6 to 8 servings

Main Courses

Porcini-Dusted Salmon with Wild Mushroom Ragout

Dried mushrooms are most often reconstituted in warm water before using, but there is another interesting way to use them: mushroom powder. The intensely concentrated powder made from ground dried mushrooms is a versatile ingredient that may be used as a coating for fish or meat—as is done in this recipe—or stirred into risotto, added to bread dough, or any number of applications. You may, however, omit the porcini powder and serve the pan-fried salmon as is with the rich mushroom ragout.

I keep a second coffee grinder on hand just for grinding spices and mushrooms. A trick I learned from Alan Kantor at the MacCallum House in mushroom-loving Mendocino is to whir a bit of dry white rice in the grinder between uses, to help eliminate lingering odors and flavors from the previous ingredient. Wipe out the grinder with a damp paper towel.

½ ounce dried porcini

4 salmon fillet pieces (6 to 8 ounces each), skin and pin bones removed

2 tablespoons olive oil

Wild Mushroom Ragout

2 tablespoons olive oil

2 shallots, minced

1 clove garlic, minced

1 pound wild mushrooms, brushed clean, trimmed, and coarsely chopped

½ cup dry white wine, more if needed

½ cup crème fraîche or whipping cream

Salt and freshly ground black pepper

For the mushroom ragout, heat the oil in a medium skillet over medium heat. Add the shallots and garlic and cook, stirring often, until tender and aromatic, 2 to 3 minutes. Add the mushrooms and cook, stirring occasionally, until they are tender and any liquid they give off has evaporated, 8 to 10 minutes. Increase the heat to medium-high and add the wine, simmering until the liquid is almost fully reduced, 1 to 2 minutes. Add the crème fraîche and cook, stirring, until evenly blended, about 1 minute; if the mushroom mixture is quite thick, add another tablespoon or so of white wine. (If using liquid cream, you will need to reduce it for a few minutes to thicken.) Take the skillet from the heat, season to taste with salt and pepper, and set aside.

Put the dried porcini in a spice mill or coffee grinder and whir to a fine powder. Transfer the mushroom powder to a plate. Pat the salmon pieces dry with paper towels and season lightly with salt and pepper. Coat the fish on all sides with the porcini powder, patting lightly to remove excess.

Heat the oil in a large skillet, preferably nonstick, over medium-high heat. When hot, gently add the salmon to the skillet, fleshy side down, and reduce the heat to medium. Cook until the surface is lightly browned and the flesh is opaque about one-third through, 3 to 5 minutes. (While the salmon is cooking, reheat the mushroom ragout over medium heat.) Turn the fillets over and continue cooking until only a touch of translucency remains in the center, 3 to 5 minutes longer, depending on the thickness of the fish.

To serve, set the salmon pieces on individual plates, spoon some of the warm mushroom ragout alongside, and serve.

Makes 4 servings

Pumpkin Gnocchi with Wild Mushroom-Sage Cream Sauce

When fresh pumpkins are available, you may bake and purée a chunk for use in this recipe, though canned pumpkin is an easy and tasty alternative. Be sure to buy the pure pumpkin purée, not the type that's preseasoned for pie filling. Black trumpet mushrooms are a particularly good choice for this recipe, their dark color and firm texture an ideal contrast to the soft gnocchi. But you could use any type with delicious results.

¼ cup unsalted butter	Salt and freshly ground black pepper
2 tablespoons thinly sliced sage	½ cup whipping cream
¾ to 1 pound wild mushrooms, brushed clean, trimmed, and sliced	Shaved or grated Parmesan cheese, for serving

Pumpkin Gnocchi

2 large russet potatoes
  (about 1½ pounds total)
1 cup pumpkin purée

¾ cup all-purpose flour
1½ teaspoons salt
1 egg

For the pumpkin gnocchi, put the potatoes in a large pan of cold water, bring to a boil over high heat, then reduce the heat to medium and simmer until the potatoes are quite tender when pierced with the tip of a knife, about 45 minutes. Drain and let cool slightly, then peel and discard the skin. While still warm, press the potatoes through a ricer or food mill into a large bowl. Stir in the pumpkin purée followed by the flour and salt, then add the egg, mixing well. Let the gnocchi dough sit for about 30 minutes.

Bring a large pot of salted water to a boil while forming the gnocchi.

Scoop about one-quarter of the gnocchi dough onto a lightly floured work surface. Roll it into a cylinder about ¾ inch thick and cut across into 1-inch pieces. Use the tines of a fork to gently roll each piece, making light grooves all the way around; dip the fork in flour as needed to avoid sticking. Continue with the rest of the gnocchi dough.

When the water has reached a rolling boil, add 20 or so gnocchi and cook until all of the gnocchi have risen to the surface, 1 to 2 minutes. Scoop them out with a large slotted spoon and set aside in a colander while cooking the remaining gnocchi. (The gnocchi can be made a few hours in advance and refrigerated, but toss lightly in olive oil while still warm to avoid sticking.)

Melt the butter in a large skillet over medium heat until very lightly browned and slightly nutty smelling. Add the sage and stir quickly just until lightly crisped and aromatic, about 30 seconds. Add the mushrooms and sauté until tender and any liquid they give off has evaporated, 5 to 8 minutes. Season with a good pinch of salt and pepper, then add the cream and bring just to a boil. Add the gnocchi and toss to evenly coat and reheat them. Spoon the gnocchi into individual shallow bowls, top with the cheese, and serve right away.

Makes 4 servings

Veal Chops with Morels and Fava Beans

Fava beans rank up there with asparagus, morels, and fresh halibut as some of the most delicious harbingers of springtime. If you're unable to find favas, you may use other fresh beans such as limas or even tender green beans. Other wild mushrooms may be used in place of the morels as well, preferably tender mushrooms such as oyster or chanterelle.

Veal chops come in two types: loin chops and rib chops. Loin chops tend to be thicker than rib chops and have a sort of T-bone shape, requiring more cooking than rib chops do; reduce the cooking time a bit if using rib chops. The morel/fava finish also would be delicious with sautéed veal escalopes that have been lightly coated in flour and pan-fried until golden brown. Or try the combination with pan-seared halibut fillet for equally tasty results.

1½ pounds whole fava beans
4 veal loin chops,
    about 1½ inches thick
Salt and freshly ground
    black pepper
2 tablespoons olive oil

2 tablespoons minced shallot or onion
6 ounces morel mushrooms, brushed
    clean, trimmed, and sliced
½ cup whipping cream
1 tablespoon minced flat-leaf
    (Italian) parsley

Remove the beans from the fava shells, pulling the stem end away along with the stringy fiber that runs down the length of the shell to help separate the halves. You should have a generous 1½ cups of shelled beans.

Bring a medium pan of salted water to a boil and prepare a medium bowl of ice water. Add the fava beans to the boiling water and cook until just barely tender, 2 to 3 minutes. Drain the beans, put them in the ice water right away and let sit until fully chilled. Drain well, then peel away and discard the tough outer skin from each bean and set the peeled beans aside.

Preheat the oven to 400°F.

Season the veal chops with salt and pepper. Heat 1 tablespoon of the olive oil in a large ovenproof skillet over medium-high heat. Add the veal chops and brown well on both sides, about 5 minutes total. Transfer the skillet to the oven and cook the chops to your taste, 7 to 10 minutes for medium, 12 to 15 minutes for medium-well to well. Remove the chops to a plate and cover loosely with foil to keep warm.

Add the remaining tablespoon of olive oil to the skillet (remember to use a hot pad as the skillet handle will be very hot) and sauté the shallot over medium heat until tender and aromatic, 1 to 2 minutes. Add the sliced morels with a pinch of salt and pepper and sauté until tender and just beginning to give off their liquid, 3 to 5 minutes. Add the cream, increase the heat to medium-high, and boil until the cream is reduced by about half, 3 to 5 minutes. Add the reserved fava beans with the parsley and any liquid collected on the plate with the veal chops. Cook until warmed through and slightly thickened, about 1 minute longer. Season to taste with salt and pepper.

Arrange the veal chops on individual plates and spoon the morel and fava bean sauce partly over and around the chops. Serve right away.

Makes 4 servings

Chicken and Matsutake Papillote with Sake

The prized matsutake is luckily among the many delicious edible wild mushrooms of our region, the quality so high that many of these mushrooms are sent to Japan where they command top dollar. I was fortunate to find three beautiful specimens on a foraging trip on Washington's Olympic Peninsula, which inspired this recipe. Oyster mushrooms or chanterelles would be particularly good substitutes for the matsutakes in this recipe.

Papillote is a French term for a simple technique of cooking foods enclosed in paper. I love this method, which traps in moisture and flavor during cooking, ideal for lean and delicate ingredients, including fish. You may use foil rather than paper, skipping the step of cutting the heart shape. Simply arrange the ingredients on one half of the foil, fold the top piece over and double-fold the three open sides to fully enclose. This doesn't have the same visual appeal of the paper packet, however.

1 bunch green onions, trimmed
¼ cup sake
1 tablespoon soy sauce
2 boneless, skinless chicken breasts
   (about 8 ounces each)

2 ounces matsutake mushrooms,
   brushed clean, trimmed,
   and thinly sliced

Cut the green onions into about 3-inch lengths, then cut those pieces lengthwise into julienne strips. Put the green onion strips in a small bowl and drizzle with the sake and soy sauce. Toss gently to mix and set aside for 5 to 10 minutes.

Preheat the oven to 425°F. Cut 2 pieces of parchment paper about 18 inches long. Fold each piece in half lengthwise and trim the paper into an oversized heart shape.

Lift out about half of the green onion strips from the sake/soy mixture, allowing excess liquid to drip back into the bowl, and put them on one half of a parchment paper heart, just in from the folded edge. Set a chicken breast over the green onions. Repeat for the second sheet of parchment. Drizzle the remaining sake/soy mixture evenly over the chicken breasts, then lay the matsutake slices on top.

For each packet, fold the other half of the parchment heart over the chicken breast. Starting at the top of the heart at the folded edge, begin making short folds that overlap slightly, working all around the open cut edges to fully seal them. If the edge doesn't seem well-sealed, and you have ample paper, you can go back around and do the same again.

Set the parchment packets on a baking sheet and bake for 18 minutes. Take the pan from the oven and carefully transfer the packets to individual plates. Either snip open the top of the packet with kitchen shears or simply tear the packet open with your fingers, careful to avoid that first puff of hot steam that will rise up along with the wonderful cooking aromas.

Makes 2 servings

A Matsutake Moment

My first foray for wild mushrooms came on Washington's Olympic Peninsula one gray, slightly damp, chill weekend in early October. I'd signed up for "The Ecology of Mushrooms," an annual offering at the Olympic Park Institute on Lake Crescent, wishing to get my feet wet (if not a little muddy too) in the world of mushroom foraging. Fred Rhoades, a lecturer at Western Washington University, leads the weekend, complete with a mini lab session looking at mushrooms under microscopes, learning about the intricate biology of mushrooms in the wild, and even a great slide show featuring some of the outstanding 3-D images he's taken over the years. But the highlight of the weekend, for me, was the two days of forays into the surrounding forest, learning to pick out the telltale signs of wild mushroom growth amid the busy distraction of things to look at on the forest floor. My sights were set on finding myself a matsutake, one of the most desirable mushrooms out there. So what if where we'd be foraging was not prime matsutake area? I didn't let that alter my goal.

Saturday, our first day out, was moderately fruitful, the twenty of us just becoming accustomed to the terrain and the keen eye it takes to pick out the mushrooms from the undergrowth. We gathered a handful of specimens to take back, including some "choice edibles" such as woodland russula *(Russula xerampelina),* delicious milk caps *(Lactarius deliciosus),* and hedgehogs *(Hydnum repandum)*—enough to sauté up (guess who played chef?) as a side dish to the night's delicious lasagna dinner.

Come Sunday, we're old pros. We head out in twos or threes to see what we can spot in this second foraging area, a bit higher elevation than Saturday's outing. Among the highlights was a stunning, huge cauliflower mushroom on which was perched, for a while, a vivid green tree frog that seemed perplexed by the attention. I was still on the prowl for my matsutake, having been foiled many times by the similar looking but fully

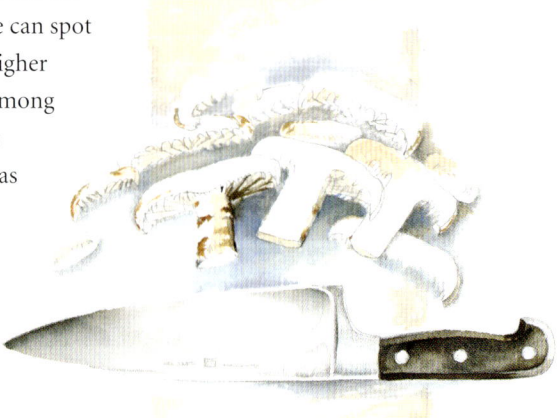

uninteresting short-stemmed russula *(Russula brevipes)*. My zigzag route took me around the base of most big trees in the area, until finally I saw the little white caps barely poking out of the ground beneath a huge tree. The stem didn't break easily like chalk, which the russula's does. My heart raced a bit; I wasn't certain that this was what I'd been after but I wanted to believe it was. I'd found three mushrooms in a cluster, of slightly varying sizes, all in ideal condition (i.e., young and unblemished).

I quietly joined the group back at the campground and we laid out our harvest. Rhoades beamed right away and exclaimed, "You found them!" He seemed nearly as pleased as I was. Back home with my treasures, I thinly sliced the mushrooms and laid them over chicken breasts, cooked in parchment paper with a touch of sake and soy sauce. It was one of the most deliciously simple things I'd tasted in some time, made more special by the reward of a mushroom hunt gone well. You'll find that recipe on page 68.

Lamb Stew with Porcini and Rosemary

This recipe is an ideal use for dried porcini mushrooms. Their concentrated flavor permeates the stew, and the flavorful soaking liquid adds depth to the dish. Dried and fresh together offers the best of both worlds; when fresh porcini are not available, the dried porcini will contribute their earthy-wild flavor while regular button mushrooms add volume. If you find lamb cheeks available, they're a great alternative to the lamb stew meat used here, not much more expensive, and they come in perfect bite-size pieces, ready to use.

½ to 1 ounce dried porcini mushrooms
   (optional)
2 to 3 cups chicken stock or beef stock
¼ cup olive oil
2 pounds lamb stew meat (such as
   shoulder), cut into 1-inch cubes
Salt and freshly ground black pepper
2 large leeks, white and pale green
   parts only, split, cleaned, and sliced

⅓ cup all-purpose flour
1 large russet potato, peeled
   and cut into 1-inch cubes
1 tablespoon minced fresh rosemary
   or 1 teaspoon dried rosemary,
   well crushed
¾ pound fresh porcini mushrooms,
   brushed clean, trimmed, and
   coarsely chopped

If using dried mushrooms, put them in a small bowl and cover with about 1 cup of boiling water. Set aside until softened and cool, about 30 minutes. Drain the mushrooms, reserving the liquid. Coarsely chop the mushrooms and set aside. Add enough stock to the soaking liquid to make 3 cups.

Heat the olive oil in a Dutch oven or other large heavy pot over medium-high heat. Season the lamb pieces with salt and pepper and, working in 2 or 3 batches, brown the lamb well on all sides, 5 to 7 minutes. Take the last batch of meat from the pot, add the leeks and cook, stirring, until they are tender and aromatic, 2 to 3 minutes. Return all the meat to the pot with any juices that have collected and sprinkle with the flour and a generous pinch of salt and pepper, stirring to evenly coat the meat. Pour in the stock (or stock/mushroom mixture) and stir in the potato and rosemary. Cover the pot and reduce the heat to medium-low. Simmer gently until the lamb is nearly tender, about 1½ hours. Stir in the fresh and dried porcini and continue cooking just until the mushrooms and lamb are tender, about 30 minutes longer. Check the seasoning, adding more salt or pepper to taste.

Spoon the stew into individual bowls and serve right away.

Makes 4 to 6 servings

Chanterelle and Chicken Pot Pie

This recipe is a great way to use leftover roasted chicken. Simply cut away all extra meat from the bones and dice it. (If you don't have enough meat, bake or poach an extra boneless chicken breast or two.) You may then simmer the chicken bones to make a simple stock for the filling. Otherwise, simmer 1½ pounds of boneless, skinless chicken breast or thigh meat in water with sliced carrots, celery, and onion, herbs, and a teaspoon of black peppercorns. Reserve the cooking liquids for the filling.

4 tablespoons unsalted butter

1 onion, finely chopped

1 cup thinly sliced carrots

1 pound chanterelles or other wild
   mushrooms, brushed clean,
   trimmed, and sliced

½ cup all-purpose flour

2 cups chicken cooking liquids or
   chicken stock

3 cups diced cooked chicken

1 cup frozen petite peas

½ cup whipping cream or
   half-and-half

2 tablespoons minced flat-leaf
   (Italian) parsley

2 tablespoons dry sherry

Salt and freshly ground
   black pepper

Pot Pie Topping

1 cup all-purpose flour

2 teaspoons minced flat-leaf
   (Italian) parsley

¼ teaspoon salt

5 tablespoons unsalted butter,
   cut into pieces and chilled

2 to 3 tablespoons ice water

1 egg (for glaze)

For the pie topping, combine the flour, parsley, and salt in a food processor and pulse once to mix. Add the chilled butter pieces and pulse to finely chop the butter until the mixture has a coarse sandy texture. Drizzle the water into the dough 1 tablespoon at a time, again pulsing briefly a few times to just blend in the water. (Alternatively, combine the flour, parsley, and salt in a large bowl and use a pastry cutter or two table knives to cut the butter into the flour mixture. Drizzle the water over, stirring with a fork to mix until a cohesive dough is formed.) It's important not to overmix the dough or it will be tough rather than flaky. The dough will not form a ball in the machine, but has the proper amount of liquid if when squeezing some of the dough between your fingers, it feels neither dusty dry nor sticky. Turn the dough out onto the work surface, form it into a ball, and wrap it in plastic. Refrigerate the dough for at least 30 minutes before rolling it out.

Preheat the oven to 400°F. Butter a 2-quart baking dish or individual ovenproof dishes.

Melt the butter in a sauté pan or large skillet over medium heat. Add the onion and carrot and sauté until tender and aromatic, 3 to 5 minutes. Add the mushrooms and cook, stirring occasionally, until tender and any liquid they give off has evaporated, 5 to 7 minutes. Sprinkle the flour over the mixture and cook for 2 minutes, stirring constantly. Slowly pour in the cooking liquids, stirring to dissolve the flour. Increase the heat to medium-high and cook, stirring often, until the sauce begins to thicken, 2 to 3 minutes. Reduce the heat to medium-low and stir in the chicken, peas, cream, parsley, and sherry. Season the filling to taste with salt and pepper. Cook for 5 minutes longer, stirring often, then take the pan from the heat and set aside.

Roll out the pot pie topping on a lightly floured work surface to about ¼ inch thick. Trim the dough into a shape that will just cover the filling in the baking dish(es). Spoon the chicken and mushroom filling into the baking dish(es) and lay the pastry topping over. If you like, any excess dough can be cut into decorative shapes for topping the pot pie(s).

In a small dish, beat the egg with 2 teaspoons of water and a pinch of salt. Brush the top of the pastry lightly with the egg wash, arrange any pastry decorations on top, and lightly brush them with egg wash as well. Put the dish(es) on a rimmed baking sheet and bake until the pastry is nicely browned and the filling is bubbling around the edges, about 20 minutes for individual dishes, about 30 minutes for one large dish. Let the pot pie cool for about 10 minutes before serving.

Makes 4 to 6 servings

Forest Cannelloni with Roasted Red Pepper Sauce

Making pasta at home may sound like a daunting task, but it's really pretty easy. You simply blend eggs and flour (with a bit of salt for flavor) to make the dough, let it rest a bit, and roll it out. A pasta machine—whether the simple hand-crank type like I use or a motorized version—makes easy work of rolling and cutting the dough, after which the pasta is ready to cook and enjoy. For a shortcut, you may instead use lasagna noodles and boil them until al dente, then cut them into about 5-inch lengths to use in place of the fresh pasta sheets made here.

The roasted red pepper sauce will be more deeply flavored if made a day in advance, which also divides the workload.

¾ pound lean ground pork

4 ounces bulk Italian-style
   pork sausage

1½ pounds fresh wild mushrooms,
   brushed clean, trimmed, and sliced,

or 1 pound fresh and 1 ounce
   dried mushrooms

15 ounces part-skim ricotta cheese

½ cup grated Parmesan cheese

Roasted Red Pepper Sauce

3 red bell peppers

2 tablespoons olive oil

1 onion, finely chopped

3 cloves garlic, chopped

2 cans (15 ounces each) diced tomatoes

2 teaspoons fresh thyme or
   ½ teaspoon dried thyme

1 bay leaf

Salt and freshly ground black pepper

Pasta Dough

1¼ cups all-purpose flour, plus more
   for rolling out pasta

½ teaspoon salt

2 eggs

For the sauce, roast the red peppers over a gas flame or under the broiler until the skin blackens, turning occasionally to roast evenly, about 10 minutes total. Put the peppers in a plastic bag, securely seal it, and set aside to cool. When cool enough to handle, peel away and discard the skin. Remove the core and seeds and chop the peppers.

Heat the oil in a large, heavy saucepan over medium heat. Add the onion and garlic and cook, stirring, until tender and aromatic, 5 to 7 minutes. Add the tomatoes with their liquid, the roasted peppers, thyme, and bay leaf with a good pinch of salt and pepper. Simmer until the sauce is slightly thickened and aromatic, about 45 minutes, stirring often and reducing the heat to medium-low once the liquids come to a boil.

While the sauce simmers, make the pasta dough. Put the flour and salt in a food processor and pulse once to blend. Add the eggs and pulse to evenly blend. Transfer the dough to the counter, form it into a ball, and knead it for a few minutes to create a satiny dough. Wrap the dough in plastic and set aside on the counter (don't refrigerate) for about 30 minutes.

When the sauce is slightly thickened, take the pan from the heat, pick the bay leaf out of the pot, and discard it. Using an immersion blender, purée the sauce until nearly smooth but still with a bit of texture. (Alternatively, purée the sauce in batches in a food processor or blender.) Season the sauce to taste with salt and pepper; set aside.

Combine the ground pork and pork sausage meat in a large skillet and sauté over medium-high heat until the meat is cooked through, 8 to 10 minutes, breaking the meat into pieces as it cooks. Scoop the meat out with a slotted spoon into a large bowl and set aside. Discard all but about 2 tablespoons of fat from the skillet, add the mushrooms, and sauté until tender and any liquid they give off has evaporated, 5 to 7 minutes. Add the mushrooms to the bowl with the pork and let cool. When cool, add the ricotta and Parmesan cheeses with about 1 cup of the red pepper sauce. Stir to evenly mix, then season the filling to taste with salt and pepper.

Cut the pasta dough in half. Flatten one half with the heel of your hand, lightly dust it with flour, and roll it through the widest rollers of a pasta machine. Fold the ends inward so that the packet is about 4 inches across, then run the pasta through the rollers again, folded-edge first. Repeat this process 6 to 8 more times to further knead the dough and make it very smooth, dusting the dough lightly with flour as needed. Decrease the roller width by one setting and pass the full length of the pasta sheet through the rollers. Continue rolling out the dough at thinner and thinner settings until the dough is about $1/16$ inch thick. Drape the pasta on a pasta rack or over the back of a chair that's been covered with a dishcloth. Repeat the rolling process with the remaining dough. Let the dough sheets sit for about 10 minutes before continuing.

Preheat the oven to 375°F. Spread about 1 cup of the sauce evenly over the bottom of a 9-by-13-inch baking dish.

Bring a large pot of well-salted water to a boil. Trim the pasta sheets into pieces about 5 inches square; you should have 12 squares. When the water's at a full rolling boil, add the pasta squares and boil until just al dente, about 1 minute. Drain the pasta and run cold water over to cool, then lay the pasta out on paper towels.

Lay a pasta square on the work surface and spoon a scant ½ cup of the filling evenly across the center. Roll the pasta edges over the filling and set the cannelloni seam-side down in the prepared baking dish. Continue with the remaining pasta and filling. When the dish is filled, pour the remaining sauce over evenly. Bake until the cannelloni are heated through, about 30 minutes. Let sit for about 10 minutes before serving.

Makes 6 servings

Wild Wellington with Truffled Merlot Sauce

One of the all-time most elegant entrées, this mushroom-coated beef tenderloin makes a showy and delicious presentation for a special dinner. Truffle makes a wonderful addition to the sauce and mushroom coating, though it can be omitted with still-delicious results.

A thermometer reading is best for confirming the proper cooking of the beef, as the pastry obscures any tactile clues to the meat's doneness; cooking time will vary with the shape of your piece of tenderloin and with variances in oven temperatures. I'm devoted to an internal thermometer I have that remains in the meat during cooking and beeps when the designated internal temperature is reached. Be sure to let the meat rest before slicing; that step is important for allowing the juices to redistribute and for permitting the residual heat in the meat to continue the cooking process.

4 tablespoons olive oil
1 beef tenderloin (about 3½ pounds)
Salt and freshly ground black pepper
½ cup minced shallot
1 pound mixed wild mushrooms,
    brushed clean, trimmed,
    and very finely chopped
¼ cup minced flat-leaf (Italian) parsley
2 teaspoons minced thyme
2¼ cups merlot or other
    full-bodied red wine

2 sheets puff pastry, thawed
1 egg, beaten with 1 tablespoon water
12 thin slices black truffle,
    plus 1 teaspoon minced black truffle
    (optional)
1½ cups rich beef stock
¼ cup Madeira
2 tablespoons unsalted butter,
    at room temperature
2 tablespoons all-purpose flour

Rub 2 tablespoons of the oil all over the beef tenderloin and season generously with salt and pepper. Heat a large skillet over medium-high heat. When hot, add the tenderloin and brown well on all sides, about 5 minutes total. Transfer the tenderloin to a plate or platter and set aside to cool completely, reserving the skillet as it is, cooked bits and all, for making the merlot sauce later.

Heat the remaining 2 tablespoons of oil in a medium skillet over medium-high heat. Add the shallot and sauté until tender and aromatic, 1 to 2 minutes, then add the mushrooms, parsley, and 1 teaspoon of the thyme with a good pinch of salt and pepper. Cook, stirring often, until the mushrooms are tender and all the liquid that they give off during cooking has evaporated, about 5 minutes. Add ¼ cup of the red wine and continue to cook, stirring, until the liquid has again fully evaporated, 1 to 2 minutes. Transfer the mushroom mixture to a bowl, add more salt or pepper to taste, and set aside to cool.

On a lightly floured work surface, lay the 2 pastry sheets side by side. Very lightly brush some of the egg wash along the long edge, about ½ inch wide, of one of the pastry sheets and overlap the second pastry sheet by ½ inch, pressing down well on the seam to securely seal the pastry sheets into one. Roll out the puff pastry to a rectangle about 3 inches longer than the tenderloin and about 12 inches wide. Spread the cooled mushroom mixture evenly over the pastry, leaving a generous 1-inch border around the pastry edge uncovered. Lay the truffle slices, if using, lengthwise down the center and set the tenderloin on top of the mushrooms.

Brush the exposed outer edge of pastry lightly with the beaten egg mixture. Draw up the long edges over the tenderloin and overlap slightly to fully enclose it in the mushroom-covered pastry, firmly pressing and pinching the seam to seal it. Fold in both ends, again pressing and pinching to fully seal the edges.

Carefully roll the pastry-wrapped tenderloin over so that the seam is on the bottom, and brush away any excess flour. Line a heavy baking sheet with parchment paper or foil and lightly oil it. Transfer the tenderloin to the baking sheet, brush the pastry evenly with some of the beaten egg, and refrigerate for at least 1 hour before cooking. (You may use some pastry trimmings, if there are any, to make decorative embellishments on top of the pastry-wrapped tenderloin, whether simple thin strips or leaf or flower cutouts.)

When ready to cook the tenderloin, preheat the oven to 450°F. Transfer the baking sheet directly to the oven and bake until the pastry is nicely browned and the internal temperature of the beef reaches 135°F for medium-rare, about 30 minutes, or 140°F for medium, about 40 minutes. If the pastry is well browned before the meat is cooked, loosely cover the Wellington with foil.

While the Wellington is baking, make the merlot sauce. Return the large skillet in which the tenderloin was seared to medium-high heat. Add the remaining 2 cups of merlot to the

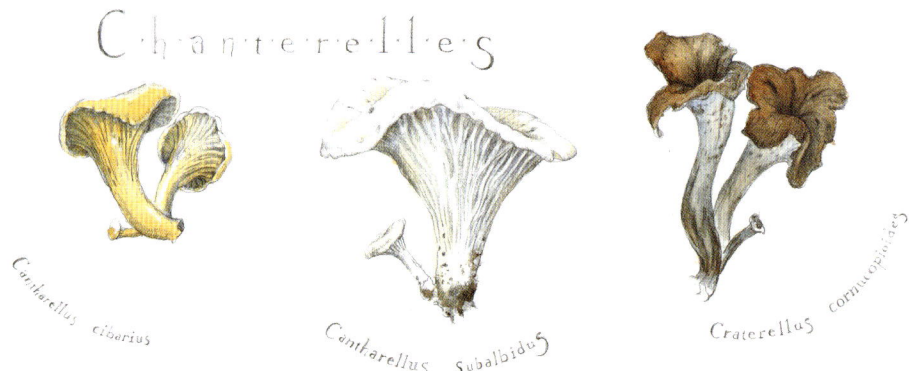

Chanterelles

Cantharellus cibarius

Cantharellus subalbidus

Craterellus cornucopioides

skillet and bring to a boil, stirring to remove any cooked bits from the bottom of the skillet. Boil the wine until it is reduced by half, about 5 minutes. Add the beef stock and Madeira and once again boil to reduce by half, 5 to 7 minutes longer. While reducing, combine the butter and flour in a small bowl and stir well to make a smooth paste.

Reduce the heat to medium-low, add the remaining thyme and the minced truffle, and gradually whisk in the butter-flour mixture, whisking constantly as it cooks until thickened, 3 to 5 minutes. Season the sauce to taste with salt and pepper and keep warm over low heat.

Take the beef Wellington from the oven, carefully transfer it to a cutting board and let sit for 10 minutes, loosely covered with foil to keep warm. Cut the Wellington into slices about 1 inch thick. Arrange 2 slices on each plate, spoon the truffled merlot sauce around, and serve right away. Alternatively, present the beef Wellington on a platter and cut it at the table, passing the warmed sauce separately.

Makes 6 to 8 servings

Sole with Wild Mushroom Stuffing and Parsley Sauce

This savory recipe is based on one of my final exam dishes from cooking school. For that dreaded "market basket" exam, each student was given a different collection of ingredients with which we needed to produce three dishes. Sole and mushrooms were in my baskets, from which I made rolled-up packets similar to those in this recipe. Cut across into pinwheel rounds, the servings are striking, set off by the brilliant green of the parsley sauce. Any kind of wild mushroom serves well in this dish.

Sole, a much smaller flatfish cousin of the celebrated Northwest halibut, comes in many varieties. Petrale sole is my favorite, offering slightly larger and firmer fillets than other delicate kinds of sole.

¾ pound wild mushrooms,
   brushed clean, trimmed,
   and coarsely chopped
½ cup minced leek or onion
2 tablespoons minced chives

1 tablespoon olive oil
Salt and freshly ground black pepper
6 sole fillets (about 1½ pounds total)
½ cup dry vermouth or
   dry white wine

Parsley Sauce

2 tablespoons unsalted butter
¼ cup minced leek or onion
2 cups fish stock
¼ cup dry vermouth or dry white wine

1 cup lightly packed flat-leaf (Italian)
   parsley leaves
¼ cup whipping cream

Combine the mushrooms, ¼ cup of the leeks, and the chives in a food processor and pulse until the mushrooms are very finely chopped. Heat the olive oil in a medium skillet over medium heat, add the mushroom mixture and cook, stirring often, until the mushrooms are tender and any liquid they give off has evaporated, about 5 minutes. Season to taste with salt and pepper. Cook a few minutes longer until the mixture is quite dry; set aside to cool.

For the parsley sauce, melt the butter in a small saucepan over medium heat. Add the leek and cook until tender and aromatic, 2 to 3 minutes. Add the fish stock, increase the heat to medium-high and simmer until the liquid is reduced by half, about 15 minutes. Add the vermouth and continue simmering until reduced again by half, about 5 to 8 minutes. Add the parsley leaves and cook, stirring, just until the leaves are tender and vivid green, 30 to 60 seconds. Transfer the mixture to a blender or food processor and purée until smooth. Return the sauce to the saucepan, stir in the cream, and season to taste with salt and pepper; keep warm over very low heat.

Preheat the oven to 400°F. Generously butter a medium baking dish.

Lay a sole fillet on the work surface with the smoother side up. Spread about 2 tablespoons of the mushroom mixture over the fillet and roll it up, beginning at the thinnest end of the fillet. Set the roll in the baking dish, seam side down, and continue with the remaining fillets and filling. Scatter the remaining ¼ cup of leeks over and around the sole packets, pour the vermouth into the baking dish, and top the fish loosely with a buttered piece of foil. Bake until the fish is just opaque through (cut into one packet to check), 12 to 15 minutes.

To serve, cut each sole packet across into 1-inch rounds. Spoon the warm parsley sauce onto individual plates, top with the sole rounds, and serve right away.

Makes 6 servings

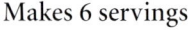

Spiced Duck Breast with Marsala Mushrooms

Gamy meats are perfect partners for the distinctive flavor of wild mushrooms. Here a pan-roasted duck breast makes way for a simple mushroom embellishment cooked in the same skillet. Just add some boiled potatoes and a crisp salad alongside, and you're set. Most any wild mushroom could be used in this recipe, but especially appropriate are the heartier, more flavorful types—such as porcini, lobster, or morel—that will hold up to the flavors of the duck and marsala.

Off-season, dried wild mushrooms are a good option. Rather than using only dried mushrooms, however, I would suggest using 6 to 8 ounces of sliced cultivated mushrooms for texture and volume, adding ½ ounce dried mushrooms (reconstituted and finely chopped) with the marsala and brandy. You could add some of the mushroom soaking liquid to the sauce with the cream, reducing it longer to reach the coating consistency.

4 small duck breasts
  (about 8 ounces each)
½ teaspoon ground allspice
½ teaspoon ground cloves
Salt and freshly ground black pepper
8 ounces wild mushrooms, brushed
  clean, trimmed, and sliced

2 tablespoons finely minced onion
  or shallot
¾ cup marsala
2 tablespoons brandy
¼ cup whipping cream
½ teaspoon minced thyme

Preheat the oven to 375°F.

Using a small sharp knife, make shallow slashes in the skin side of the duck breasts in a diamond pattern, not quite to the flesh. Sprinkle the skin with the allspice and cloves and season liberally with salt and pepper. Heat a heavy ovenproof skillet, preferably cast iron, over medium-high heat. When hot, add the duck breasts skin-side down and cook until lightly browned and the fat begins to render, 2 to 3 minutes. Transfer the skillet to the oven and roast for 3 minutes longer, then carefully turn the breasts over and continue cooking until the breasts are medium, soft pink in the center, 3 to 5 minutes longer. Take the skillet from the oven, set the breasts aside on a cutting board, and cover with foil to keep warm.

While the duck is resting, prepare the mushrooms. Spoon off and discard all but about 2 tablespoons of the fat from the skillet. Add the mushrooms and onion and cook over medium heat, stirring often, until the mushrooms are tender, 3 to 5 minutes. Add the marsala and brandy, increase the heat to high, and cook until the liquid is reduced by half, about 5 minutes. Add the cream and thyme and continue to reduce until the sauce has a coating consistency, 1 to 2 minutes longer. Season to taste with salt and pepper.

To serve, cut each of the duck breasts into slices at a slight angle, about ¾ inch thick, and arrange them in a fan on individual plates. Spoon the marsala mushrooms over and serve right away.

Makes 4 servings

Uptown Macaroni and Cheese

One of the best dishes of macaroni and cheese I ever made would be hard to reproduce exactly, made from a collection of four or five different types of cheeses that lingered in the refrigerator, remnants of an after-dinner cheese plate from a dinner party. That experience made me realize that as good as plain old cheddar mac is, the result is far more compelling when a variety of cheeses is used; feel free to alter the selections here to suit your taste and what's in your refrigerator. Add a fancy little mesclun salad alongside, open a lovely bottle of red wine, and enjoy the best macaroni and cheese you've had in years! Most any type of wild mushroom may be used in place of the porcini. This recipe is baked in individual ramekins, though you could also bake it in a 1½-quart baking dish instead.

8 to 12 ounces porcini mushrooms, brushed clean, trimmed, and finely chopped, or 2 ounces dried porcini

2½ cups dry macaroni

3 cups milk

1 slice onion

2 bay leaves

1 teaspoon whole black peppercorns

6 tablespoons unsalted butter

Salt and freshly ground black pepper

¼ cup all-purpose flour

6 ounces sharp white cheddar cheese, grated

4 ounces fontina cheese, finely chopped

4 ounces St. Nectaire cheese, finely chopped

4 ounces Asiago cheese, grated

½ cup chopped green onion or ¼ cup chopped chives

⅓ cup fresh bread crumbs

If using dried mushrooms, put them in a small bowl and pour about 1 cup boiling water over. Set aside until tender and cool, about 30 minutes. Drain the mushrooms, discarding the liquid or saving it for another use. Finely chop the mushrooms and set aside.

Bring a large pot of salted water to a boil over high heat. Stir in the macaroni, reduce the heat to medium-high and cook until the macaroni is tender to the bite, about 10 minutes. Drain well and set aside, tossing the pasta from time to time as it cools so it doesn't stick together.

Put the milk in a small saucepan with the onion slice, bay leaves, and peppercorns. Bring just to a low boil over medium heat, then take the pan from the heat and let sit to infuse for 10 to 15 minutes.

While the milk is infusing, melt 2 tablespoons of the butter in a medium skillet over medium-high heat. Add the fresh porcinis and sauté, stirring occasionally, until the mushrooms are tender and any liquid they give off has evaporated, 5 to 7 minutes. Season lightly with salt and pepper; set aside.

Preheat the oven to 350°F. Generously butter six 8-ounce ramekins or other individual baking dishes.

Melt the remaining 4 tablespoons of the butter in a large saucepan over medium heat. Whisk in the flour and cook, whisking constantly, until the mixture foams up and has a very slightly toasty smell (it should not brown), 2 to 3 minutes. Slowly whisk in the warm milk, leaving the aromatics behind in the bottom of the pan. Continue to cook the sauce, whisking often, until it thickens, 8 to 10 minutes. Gradually whisk in the cheeses until they are fully incorporated and melted. Season the sauce to taste with salt and pepper, then add the macaroni and stir with a wooden spoon to fully coat all the pasta with the cheese sauce. Add the cooked fresh or reconstituted dried porcinis with the green onion and stir to evenly blend.

Spoon the macaroni mixture into the prepared ramekins and sprinkle the bread crumbs evenly over. Set the ramekins on a baking sheet and bake until the macaroni and cheese is bubbling hot and the tops are nicely browned, 20 to 25 minutes. Let sit for a few minutes before setting on individual plates to serve.

Makes 6 servings

Northwest Truffles

It may be culinary blasphemy, but I admit to not being the most ardent fan of truffles. Yes, they're rare, nearly mythic, and uniquely aromatic, but for the price I'd just as soon have the same dollar value of porcini or matsutakes or morels. Having confessed that, I do nonetheless appreciate the refined gastronomic elegance that only a truffle can provide. I've been lucky enough to have two outstanding, memorable truffle experiences that serve as high benchmarks of truffle greatness.

The first of these extravaganzas was at Gérard Boyer's 3-star restaurant, Les Crayères, in the Champagne region of France. It was early December and truffles were abundant in the area and on the menu. We chose two indulgent preparations, the most mind-blowing of them the simplest: A whole wheel of exceptional Brie (probably Brie de Meaux, but I don't recall for certain) had been halved horizontally, thin slices of truffle arranged evenly over the exposed cheese before the halves were sandwiched back together. I suspect this was done at least a day before serving; the degree to which the essence of the truffle infused the thin wedge of cheese was astonishing.

A memorable meal, to be sure (and that was just the cheese course), but it has since been matched by the January "Truffle Treasure" dinner I indulged in not long ago at The Herbfarm restaurant in Woodinville, Washington. We sampled no less than four different varieties of truffle in one sitting, beginning with side-by-side truffle tarts as part of the first course: one with the Périgord black truffle *(Tuber melanosporum)* from France, the other topped with Oregon's little-known brown truffle (nomenclature unknown). Next came delicate ravioli with a filling of celery root and Oregon white truffles *(Tuber gibbosum)*, ethereal and perfect, followed by seared foie gras with Périgord truffles and Yellow Finn potatoes. My favorite by far was the thyme-grilled squab with Oregon black truffles *(Leucangium carthusiana)*, lentils, and golden beets. (Note that The Herbfarm also features a Mycologist's Dream menu in October, which I can also attest is a worthy indulgence for mushroom lovers.)

I find—as do many truffle fans—that Oregon truffles are on par with those from Périgord or Italy's Piedmont region. And these truffles do have quite a following, evidenced by the North American Truffling Society that calls Corvallis, Oregon, home. President of the society, while I write this book, is Dr. Charles Lefevre, who earned his doctorate in forest science, within the mycology program, at Oregon State University. In 1999, he founded New World Truffieres, Inc., selling seedlings of trees preinoculated with truffle spores. To date, he's sold many thousands of the trees to wholesale customers along the West Coast and as far away as Virginia.

"The Northwest has such a wealth of culinary treasures," Lefevre says. "To add truffles to the selection just seems very natural. Along with the great foods and wines here, truffles imbue a certain prestige to the region." Some, though, would argue that Northwest truffles don't live up to the quality of their European kin, a bad rap that Lefevre clearly finds frustrating. It's not that the region's truffle varieties are of any lesser quality, as he explains it, but perhaps they suffer from inconsistent quality due to harvesting practices.

In Europe, pigs or dogs are used to find truffles, which give off an unmistakable aroma that the animals track down for us olfactorally challenged humans. Here, however, foragers look for an array of cues—from forest characteristics to evidence of animal activity—and rake in a likely truffle patch to harvest whatever truffles there are. The hitch is that truffles within one patch ripen at different rates, so this method can unearth underripe and ripe specimens, which Lefevre likens to picking all the tomatoes from a plant when only one or two are fully ripe. The European method is more selective since truffles don't acquire their powerful, soil-permeating aroma until they reach maturity. Without fully developed character, it's natural that a too-young truffle—like a firm, green tomato—would prove unsatisfying. An aromatic truffle is ideal to eat. But without aroma, a truffle still may have potential. Unfortunately, this potential is hard to decipher without cutting into the truffle. If the interior is solid white, no color variance or marbling, it's far too immature to offer any flavor or aroma. If, however, the flesh is tan-to-light-brown (for white truffles) or smoky gray (for black truffles) with visible marbling, the truffle will develop more aroma and flavor after a few days in the refrigerator, in a heavy paper bag or wrapped in a dry paper towel stored in a plastic container.

So, how does the truffle master most like to enjoy his truffles? "I inhale them," says Lefevre with a laugh, hinting that a good lungful of the complex musty aroma can be satisfying in itself. Culinarily speaking, he prefers to keep things really simple, adding truffle to a classic risotto, creamy pasta, or a perfectly plain omelet. In that vein, my recipe for Deviled Eggs, made with Oregon white truffles in mind, is on page 36.

Cooking with Wild Mushrooms

Buying and Storing Wild Mushrooms

When you're walking through the market and see a basket filled with plump morels or big beautiful chanterelles, don't say to yourself "Hmmm, nice. I'll come back in another week or two and pick up a pound," because a quick turn in the weather can bring an end to the season without warning. While supplies are not always quite that precarious, it pays to be opportunistic when it comes to cooking wild mushrooms. Work them into your menu plans while they're available and avoid being too frustrated when they aren't, relishing instead that there are some things in our too-predictable world that still are truly at the whims of nature.

Since wild mushrooms come in a variety of forms, no single standard of shopping tips covers them all, but start off by choosing mushrooms that are free of blemishes such as cuts or dry, wrinkly spots. The mushroom should look plump and relatively even across its surface area. Mushrooms generally have a clean and earthy aroma when perfect and fresh, but begin taking on a sharper, vaguely ammonia-like odor as they start to go bad. Also avoid mushrooms that have a slimy surface (some mushrooms, such as the slippery jack, have a naturally slimy finish but these rarely show up in retail settings) or soft spots, which typically indicate that they're beginning to spoil.

Don't be turned off by mushrooms that have a pine needle or two, bits of moss, leaves, or other forest debris on them. Those are just signs of nature that sometimes come along for the ride when wild mushrooms are collected. It'll take only a few seconds to clean them, and unless the mushroom is very dirty I prefer to do this just before cooking so the mushroom remains undisturbed as long as possible.

Wild mushrooms keep best when they're stored cool and dry. Once you get your mushrooms home, refrigerate them in a lightly closed paper bag, which protects the mushrooms from too much exposure to dehydrating cold air circulation but allows them to "breathe." Keeping moisture from accumulating is important, as it greatly advances spoilage. Plastic bags, for this reason, are not a good choice because they trap in moisture that turns mushrooms soggy rather quickly. If plastic is all you have available, loosely wrap the mushrooms first in a couple layers of paper towels, then put them into the bag and leave the bag open. Depending on how long ago the mushrooms were harvested, they may hold up for a few days or longer, though results will typically be best if you cook the mushrooms within a day or two of purchase.

Preparing Wild Mushrooms

When cleaning wild mushrooms, a "dry clean" method is best because mushrooms are like delicious little sponges, capable of absorbing quantities of water. This absorbed moisture will distort the mushroom's texture and dilute other ingredients when released during cooking.

To clean mushrooms, I use a soft-bristled pastry brush, flicking away any dirt or debris from them. Chanterelles may require a little more care in cleaning, as they sometimes have deeply indented caps that can hide a surprising amount of forest souvenirs. You can halve the mushroom first, exposing more of the deep cap for thorough cleaning. Halving is a good idea when cleaning morels, too, as their hollow stems can sometimes harbor dirt or other debris.

Another handy tool for cleaning smooth, firm mushrooms is a paper towel, which can be very lightly dampened if needed to help remove stubborn patches of dirt. Only as a last resort should you use water to clean mushrooms, and then only for the briefest of dips! Fill a large bowl with cold water and have a mat of several layers of paper towels ready alongside. Drop the mushrooms into the water and briskly swish them around in the water with your hands, just for a few seconds. Lift the mushrooms up out of the water, let drip for a moment, then lay them out in a single layer on the paper towels, gently patting with more towels to remove excess water as quickly as possible. Don't simply pour the whole bowl—water and mushrooms—through a colander, or the dirt you worked to dislodge may simply fall back onto the mushrooms again.

Some types of mushrooms—especially those with broad, meaty stems such as porcini or matsutake—can be infested with worms that crawl up through the stem to the cap. Not a very pleasant encounter, to be sure, but such is the nature of wild edibles! When preparing these mushrooms, it's a good idea to trim away the end of the stem to see whether there are any telltale vertical worm holes in the mushrooms. If so, I just keep slicing up the stem, bit by bit; sometimes the worm holes stop partway up, other times not. I've had to toss out whole, glorious porcini after finding that despite looking impeccable from the outside, there had been a feast already taking place in the cap.

When it comes to cooking mushrooms, the general rule of thumb is hot and fast—whether sautéed, deep-fried, broiled, or grilled—so that the mushrooms cook through but retain their texture and a maximum of flavor. For sautéing, it's important to not crowd the pan, or the mushrooms will give off loads of their liquid and boil to a soggy, bland mess rather than keeping their character intact. Even in ideal conditions, mushrooms give off some liquid to the skillet as they cook, but how much depends on the mushroom and the heat of the pan. Use a large enough skillet so the mushrooms are in a roomy single layer, or cook them in batches if necessary.

Just to prove there are exceptions to all rules, mushrooms do suit themselves to soups, stews, and a few other moist cooking methods. Unless using dried mushrooms (which are ideal candidates for these recipes), it's best to add the mushrooms only 30 minutes or so before a long-cooking recipe, such as a stew, is to be finished, so they'll cook through and contribute flavor without becoming too soft. Firm mushrooms that hold up well—such as porcini or cauliflower—will be better suited to moist cooking than more delicate mushrooms such as chanterelles.

Wild mushrooms should always be thoroughly cooked (until they are tender) before eating because even some of the most popular wild mushrooms contain mild toxins that can be harmful to some people but are eliminated in cooking. An exception is truffles, which are often added raw to dishes—in very thin shavings or julienned—just before serving, preserving a maximum of aroma and flavor up to the moment of eating.

Chanterelles

Cantharellus cibarius

Cantharellus subalbidus

Craterellus cornucopioides

Dried Wild Mushrooms and Other Alternatives to Fresh

Not all mushrooms dry well, but those that do are nearly as prized in their dry form as fresh. Porcini, morels, candy caps, and black trumpets are ideal candidates, offering up a pronounced concentration of flavor and aroma when reconstituted in liquid before cooking. A fringe benefit is the flavorful soaking liquid you'll have after reconstituting the mushrooms, ideal for adding to soups, stews, or sauces. Hot water is perfect for plumping the dried mushrooms, though you may use mildly flavored stock as well. Another bonus with dried mushrooms is that they're available year-round, allowing for a wild mushroom fix when fresh are unavailable.

Many mushroom fans swear by freezing some of the seasonal bounty to enjoy for months to come. The trick is to first sauté the mushrooms in a touch of butter or oil (but no seasoning) until tender and any liquid they give off has evaporated. Let the cooked mushrooms cool completely, then pack them in recipe-size portions in individual resealable bags and freeze. When ready to use the mushrooms, their texture will be best if you transfer them from the freezer to the refrigerator for slow, gradual thawing a day or so before you plan to cook them.

Home-drying is another easy option. If you have a food dehydrator, it is perfect for even, thorough mushroom drying (follow the manufacturer's instructions). It's important for the mushrooms to dry to the point of being brittle before you store them. Because air circulation is important for the drying process, an oven is not the ideal tool (though a convection oven can be used in a pinch). The temperature needs to be very low (about 100°F to 110°F), so the moisture is drawn off gently and the mushroom doesn't become tough and hard. If the weather's dry and hot, you can even sun dry the mushrooms, setting them on wire racks on top of a dark kitchen towel in direct sun.

How long drying will take, using any method, depends on the mushroom's moisture content and how large the pieces are. Most mushrooms should be cut into thin slices, though morels can be dried whole, as can small mushrooms (candy caps are typically dried whole). Once dried, the mushrooms should still be stored in an airtight container. Tightly sealed jars are preferred by many mycologists, some of whom then store the jars in the freezer for added longevity.

This listing is just a sampling of the many wild mushroom events held throughout the Pacific Northwest region each year.

JULY

Wild Mushroom Workshops

Eagle River Nature Center
Eagle River, Alaska
907-694-2108 or www.ernc.org
During Alaska's brief but often very fruitful wild mushroom season (typically July to early September), the Eagle River Nature Center will host a handful of wild mushroom workshops. This "gateway to Chugach State Park" is just a 45-minute drive from Anchorage, an interpretive and educational center that promotes a wide range of natural studies. Specific program dates and times vary somewhat year to year, but are posted on the Web about three months in advance.

OCTOBER

Great Fall Mushroom Hunt

The Aerie Resort, Malahat, British Columbia
800-518-1933 or www.aerie.bc.ca
This event is a seemingly incongruous—but fully delightful—combination of elegant accommodations and wild mushroom foraging. Held Sundays, typically from early October through mid-November, the "hunt" begins with lunch at the resort. Then you're off with the chef and a local mushroom specialist to forage in the lush forest area nearby, learning as you go about the different varieties found in the region. Return to the resort's kitchen for a cooking demonstration using mushrooms collected on the trip.

Wild Mushroom Show

Seattle, Washington
206-522-6031 or www.psms.org
Established in 1964, this annual event put on by the Puget Sound Mycological Society offers a full weekend of cooking demonstrations, extensive displays, workshops, slide shows, mushroom arts and crafts (sometimes including paintings done with ink made from wild mushrooms!), and a book sale.

Wild Mushroom Festival

Long Beach Peninsula, Washington
800-451-2542 or
www.funbeach.com/mushroom
Every year from mid-October through mid-November, locations all along the Long Beach Peninsula host a variety of events and festivities celebrating mushrooms indigenous to the area. There are wild mushroom workshops and field excursions led by experts, prix-fixe dinners, and cooking classes. Participating restaurants, inns, and bed-and-breakfast establishments also offer daily wild mushroom specials.

Yachats Village Mushroom Fest

Yachats, Oregon
800-929-0477 or www.yachats.org
In the middle of October, the Yachats Area Chamber of Commerce (along with many cosponsors including the Lincoln County Mycological Society, the North American Truffling Society, and the Cascade Mycological

Society) sponsors a three-day festival with fabulous wild mushroom cuisine, mycologist-guided mushroom walks, exhibits, and identification by experts. There are also cooking demonstrations and fungi products for sale, plus music and entertainment.

Mount Pisgah Arboretum Mushroom Festival and Plant Sale

Eugene, Oregon

541-747-3817 or www.efn.org/~mtpisgah

This festival is held the last Sunday in October and features displays of a broad range of fungi collected throughout western Oregon and plenty of mushroom information. Experts are on hand to answer questions and help with mushroom identification, there are guided nature walks, tours of the arboretum, fresh pressed cider, music, and children's activities.

NOVEMBER

Mendocino Wine and Mushroom Fest

Mendocino, California

866-466-3636 or www.gomendo.com

Held in mid-November, this festival is a twelve-day countywide celebration with dozens of events to choose from, including winemaker dinners, cooking classes, mushroom tastings, guided mushroom walking tours, exhibits, and special featured mushroom menus. There is also a daylong symposium with lectures by mycologists and chefs, lunch, and a mushroom hunt and tasting.

David Arora's Mendocino Mushroom Foray

Albion, California

David Arora, master mycologist and author (*Mushrooms Demystified* and *All That the Rain Promises, and More . . .* , two outstanding wild

mushroom resources), teaches only sporadically, except for his annual Thanksgiving weekend foray. This event begins the day after Thanksgiving with the first of several mushroom hunts. Other activities include identification workshops and cooking demonstrations. In addition to Arora, who has a truly encyclopedic knowledge of wild mushrooms, other experienced mushroom hunters and talented chefs contribute. For more information write to him, at arora_david@yahoo.com.

DECEMBER

Camp Mushroom at Sea Ranch Lodge

Sea Ranch, California

800-SeaRanch or www.searanchlodge.com

Led by Charmoon Richardson of the Wild About Mushrooms Co. and held at the beautiful Sea Ranch Lodge, this early December weekend is packed with mushroom hunting, feasting, and education. Learn to identify mushroom habitats, determine edible from nonedible mushrooms, and ways to best cook mushrooms. Enjoy a five-course mushroom dinner, paired with wines, made from the mushrooms you gather. The group is small and participants include beginners as well as experienced hunters.

JANUARY

SOMA Winter Mushroom Camp

Navarro, California

707-887-1888 or www.somamushrooms.org/Camp/camp.html

Sponsored by the Sonoma County Mycological Association, this three-day event is held at a Boy Scout camp, usually over the Martin Luther King Day weekend, and includes expert-led hunts, classes, speakers, slide shows, workshops (from mushroom dyeing to cultivation), specimen displays, and wild mushroom meals.

MYCOLOGICAL SOCIETIES

There are dozens of mycological societies throughout the Northwest, the key among them listed here. Most offer monthly meetings as well as mushroom shows, field trips, educational seminars, and—certainly—opportunities for tasty mushroom sampling throughout the year. For information on other regional and national mushrooming groups, go to the North American Mycological Association Web site at www.namyco.org.

Mycological Society of San Francisco
www.mssf.org
North American Truffling Society
Corvallis, Oregon
www.fsl.orst.edu/mycology/NATS.HTM
Oregon Mycological Society
Portland, Oregon
www.wildmushrooms.org
Puget Sound Mycological Society
Seattle, Washington
www.psms.org

Sonoma County Mycological Association
Santa Rosa, California
www.somamushrooms.org
South Vancouver Island Mycological Society
Victoria, British Columbia
www.svims.ca
Vancouver Mycological Society, Vancouver
British Columbia
www.geocities.com/RainForest/Andes/8896

WILD MUSHROOM RESOURCES

Fungi Perfecti (www.fungi.com or 800-780-9126) in Olympia, Washington, is perhaps the most complete resource for the wild mushroom buff, particularly with regard to growing your own, from self-contained kits for shiitake or oyster mushrooms to "patches" that are touted to establish outdoor growth of morels! Also books, posters, much more.

Gourmet Mushrooms, Inc. (www.mycopia.com or 707-823-1743), sells mostly high-quality cultivated mushrooms, primarily wholesale though they offer two multi-mushroom packages, which will include foraged wild mushrooms in season.

Mendocino Mushrooms (707-964-1646), founded by Eric Schramm in 1984, provides a good range of fresh mushrooms in-season as available (including gold and black chanterelles, morels, porcini, hedgehogs, and matsutake), plus dried mushrooms (candy caps among them) throughout the year. Sales are wholesale, in large quantities.

Millard Family Mushrooms is a family operation in central coastal Oregon (www.mushroomsbymillard.net) that sells primarily dried (though some fresh, in season) local wild mushrooms in prime condition. Among varieties they feature are morels, candy caps, matsutakes, and chanterelles.

MykoWeb (www.mykoweb.com) is a great resource with photographs and information about hundreds of West Coast mushrooms, including many of the choice edibles.

Oregon White Truffles (www.oregonwhitetruffles.com) sells its namesake truffles (as well as the Oregon black truffle and a few other less common varieties).

The Truffle Zone (www.trufflezone.com) sells Oregon truffles.

Wild About Mushrooms (707-887-1888 or www.wildaboutmushrooms.net) is "dedicated to sharing the joys and benefits of wild mushrooms in a safe, enjoyable, and responsible manner." Owner Charmoon Richardson shares his expertise at many events each year, including mushroom hunts (his Oregon Cascades Foray each October is a five-day extravaganza), identification seminars, and other classes in Northern California and beyond.

BOOKS

If this cookbook has whetted your appetite and you'd like to read more about the wild mushrooms in the Pacific Northwest, these books are among the best resources:

Arora, David. *Mushrooms Demystified.* Berkeley, Calif.: Ten Speed Press, 1986.

—, *All That the Rain Promises, and More . . . : A Hip Pocket Guide to Western Mushrooms.* Berkeley, Calif.: Ten Speed Press, 1991.

Lincoff, Gary. *National Audubon Society Field Guide to North American Mushrooms.* New York: Alfred A. Knopf, 2000.

McKenny, Margaret, and Daniel E. Stuntz. *The New Savory Wild Mushroom.* Seattle: University of Washington Press, 1987.

Parker, Harriette. *Alaska's Mushrooms: A Practical Guide.* Seattle: Alaska Northwest Books, 1994.

Cantharellus cibarius